MW00412262

Ain't Life Fun!

Ain't Life Fun!

When You Focus on the Good Stuff

Clayton Poland

Thanks for having us in again this year! Blessings

Copyright © 2017 Clayton Poland
All rights reserved. No part of this publication may be reproduced, distributed,
or transmitted in any form or by any means, including photocopying,
recording, or other electronic or mechanical methods, without the prior
written permission of the publisher, except in the case of brief quotations
embodied in reviews and certain other non-commercial uses permitted by
copyright law.

Some names and details were changed to protect the privacy of the individuals
in each story.

ISBN-13: 978-1977509406
ISBN-10: 1977509401

To my loving wife Leigh. You have stuck by me through all the stories of our life. The good, the bad, and the ugly. I cannot wait to write many more amazing stories with you. I love you!

Ethan - You have always been a great young man! I cannot wait to see how you use the power of story to transform the world!

Maddie - You bring life to any room. You are a joy to be around I know your life will continue to be an inspiring story to everyone you meet!

Charlie – You provide us with new stories each and every day! Don't ever lose your smile or desire to make others laugh!

Contents

CONTENTS

<u>INTRODUCTION</u>

A Good Story

I love a good story!

In fact, my entire family loves a good story.

When was the last time you heard a really good story? If you're like me, you stored it in your memory bank, retelling it over and over again to family and friends.

Stories have the power to connect. They can drive a point home. Help someone understand and relate to you. Help you see something from a new perspective.

Stories come in all shapes and sizes: long, short, funny, and serious. Fables are a classic style of storytelling, involving animals, plants, or other objects as the main characters. Parables are allegorical stories that teach a moral principle or truth. Movies tell great stories. Ballads are short stories set to a catchy melody. Stories have the power to connect the storyteller to his or her audience. Regardless of the type or genre, I love stories!

As a child, back in the three-channel days, Sunday afternoons in rural Louisiana consisted of a matinee movie. I don't remember many of the movies that aired. However, I do remember the infomercials because they played every five minutes! A 90-minute movie would fill 4 hours. Generally, the infomercials were an advertisement for vinyl siding. I vividly remember the advertisers saying, "Vinyl siding is the new cutting-edge product that's going to revolutionize the building industry!" I was sharing this memory with a friend and he could actually remember the 1-800 number to call for more info about the vinyl siding. It's amazing how their catchy short stories connected with young boys.

One Sunday, they featured a standup comedian named Jerry Clower. HAAAWWW! Jerry Clower was a country humorist who rose to popularity in the late 70s. Jerry's style of comedy was filled with stories from his childhood adventures and misadventures with his friend Marcel Ledbetter.

My favorite story he told was about a female receptionist at a hotel where he and Marcel stayed during a tour of the Northeast. He said this lady was very memorable because "she had on so much green eye shadow that I thought her gallbladder had busted." What a word picture! Variations of this line quickly became part of my language. Jerry Clower was the quintessential Southern humorist. According to Clower, a comedian tells funny stories. While a humorist tells stories funny. Jerry's style of storytelling engaged his audiences. His recordings are a favorite of my family. The kids and I still listen to his stories even though they're nearly 40 years old.

Grandparents are another source of great stories. I remember my grandfather talking about one of his first jobs that required him to stand on his feet for hours on end. At the time, he was very poor and couldn't afford new comfortable shoes. Every day, he would go to the company restroom, fold toilet paper into his shoes, giving him a cushion to help make it through the day. My mom's mother, Mamaw Lizzie, has great stories! She tells stories of the good ole days. In fact, one of her stories is so great that she had an article written about the tale in a popular hunting magazine.

I love stories so much that a few years ago, I began to compile a journal of stories from my childhood, school days, college days, and life in general. At the time of this writing, my journal contains over 23,000 words. When I put a story in my journal, I take the Hansel and Gretel approach. I don't write down the entire story. I leave just enough breadcrumbs about the story to help my mind get back to the original story. Most of the time, a simple sentence with a dozen words will do the trick. Thus, my journal has close to one thousand stories!

One of my favorite story writers is Agatha Christie. My favorite book of hers is *And Then There Were None*, sometimes called *Ten Little Indians*. Ten strangers are invited to a mysterious island by someone they've never met named Mr. Owen. After their first meal together, they gather in the living room of the house and a record begins to play. This record details crimes that each of these ten people have committed and gotten away with. The way the fate of these individuals plays out through the remainder of the book is fascinating. I read this book at least once every couple of years. I know the story, how each part plays out, and how it will end. But it's a great story that I love to read again and again. I once heard a Hollywood director say *And Then There Were None* was the gold standard when it comes to writing a suspenseful story.

Stories connect people. They have a way of helping us remember the past, connect to the present, and dream of the future.

Ain't life fun when you focus on the good stuff! Sure, life has its share of difficulties and tragedies. But it's also filled with good stuff. Too often, we lose sight of all the good stuff in our lives, focusing only on the bad. The news and social media focus on negativity 24/7. It feels like they're allergic to the good stuff!

My family has certainly had our share of difficulties and tragedies. We've had our lights disconnected, had friends and family disappoint us and us disappoint them, been forced out of jobs, and experienced terrible heartache, including the loss of a child.

We could choose to spend every day focused on memories of the challenges, difficulties, and heartaches. Or we can focus on the good stuff. You are in complete control of your focus. As a family, we've chosen to focus on the good stuff and embrace the challenges, difficulties, and heartaches as a normal part of life.

The result – life is fun! True it's not all rainbows, unicorns, and fireworks, but it's much more fun when you choose to focus on the good stuff.

Many of the stories contained in this book are stories about our family. At the time they happened, none of us thought these stories were anything special, but as we've retold them through the years, people have been inspired to apply the principles of each story to their own families. That's my desire for you. More than simply enjoying the stories, I hope you apply their principles within your family. I know they have the power to help your family enjoy life to the fullest!

These stories aren't meant to be an in-depth scientific study on relationships, parenting, or family dynamics. There are plenty of those books written from this perspective by very qualified doctors, psychiatrists, and health professionals. I love those books. I've read a library full of them. This book is a real-life, down and dirty guide full of simple principles that have worked for our family and will work for your family as well.

These stories help you understand how we've raised three children who are self-confident but not arrogant; who have a healthy self-esteem, keeping them from being deflated when they're picked on or laughed at; and who have confidence to try new things, meet new people, and seek after all that God has for them. These stories show

how we choose to find the silver lining in the darkest of storms and raise three awesome kids who love their mom and dad and love spending time with them.

The stories in each chapter vary in length. Some takeaways are more powerful than others. Sometimes the advice will be for your kids and sometimes it'll be for you the parent. Yet, when the principles in these stories are applied, they allow any family to boldly say, "Ain't life fun when you focus on the good stuff!"

Let's go uncover some of the good stuff!

CHAPTER 1

Your Love and Approval

So God created mankind in his own image, in the image of God he created them; male and female he created them. —Genesis 1:27 (NIV)

For we are God's masterpiece. He has created us anew in Christ Jesus, so we can do the good things he planned for us long ago.
—Ephesians 2:10 (NLT)

A group of ancient monks in Thailand receives word that an invading army is about to attack their temple. This, of course, sends them into a frenzy but for a reason you might not expect. You see, the monks have a giant solid gold statue of Buddha. To protect their sacred statue from plunder, the monks cover the entire Buddha in a 12-inch-thick casing of clay and plaster, imbedding small bits of glass into the plaster to make the statue appear cheap, ordinary, and worthless.

It works because in 1767, the Burmese army invades the temple, slaughters all the monks, and ignores the clay statue. The statue remains in the temple ruins so long that everyone forgets that it is, in fact, a highly valuable golden Buddha. In the early 1800s, the president of Thailand orders every Buddha statue to be brought to a central location until new temples can be constructed to house each Buddha. This massive clay-covered golden Buddha is among those rounded up. Some accounts say this clay Buddha, because of its size, is worshiped over the next century.

In 1935, the statue is transferred to a new location but because no temple is large enough to house the clay Buddha, it's placed outside, covered only by a tin roof. This temple location is abandoned, leaving the clay Buddha outside in the elements for the next 20 years.

In 1955, the statue must be moved to make room for a new highway. Cranes and construction equipment are brought on site to load the clay Buddha onto a truck to transport it to its new location. There are many versions of what happens during the loading process, but this scenario seems the most logical. Because this Buddha is made of gold and not clay, the weight of the statue is greatly underestimated. As the crane operators begin to lift the statue, the lift ropes snap and the Buddha falls to the ground, cracking the clay casing. To make matters worse, it begins to rain. The monks rush to cover the statue to protect it until the rain stops.

During the night, the head monk goes to examine the statue to make sure it's staying dry. When he shines his light under the covering, he's surprised to see light reflecting from the clay. He examines the crack in the clay casing closer and sees what he assumes is gold. He quickly locates a hammer and chisel spending the next several hours chiseling away the clay and plaster to expose the massive Golden Buddha. Within the plaster, the monks also discover a key that allows the statue to be disassembled into nine pieces for easier transport. The next morning, the monks are elated because the statue, once considered to have little value, is realized to be the largest golden Buddha statue every constructed. It remains to this day the largest solid gold statue of any kind.

Today, the statue is on display in a new temple built in 2010 called the Temple of the Golden Buddha in Bangkok, Thailand. It's estimated the statue was built 700 years ago. The exact measurements and weights of the statue vary. The diameter is between 10 to 11 feet with a height between 13 to 16 feet. The approximate weight is between 5 and 6 tons, giving it a conservative present-day value between $200 and $250 million.

Here's what I love about this story.

We're all created in the image of God. We stand in awe of the value of this massive golden Buddha statue, but forget that Ephesians 2:10 reminds us we're God's masterpiece. Romans 5:8 adds that while we were yet sinners, Christ died for us. Meaning, while we were yet sinners, covered in clay, concrete, plaster and cheap shards of glass, Jesus willingly died for us. 1 Peter 1:18-19 tells us that we weren't redeemed with corruptible things like gold and silver, but with the blood of Christ. You are valuable! Your kids are valuable!

Sadly, just as the people of Thailand forgot about the value of the golden Buddha, we've forgotten how valuable we are. As we go through life, the invading armies of peer pressure, criticism, and self-doubt cause us to cover ourselves with cheap plaster. The plaster has been in place for so long that we've forgotten our true value. We've forgotten that we are priceless and made in the image of God. We've forgotten that we've been bought with a price. We hide our true identity from the world, living each day, adding layers of protection over our hearts and minds, hoping the world never discovers who we really are. We seek joy and happiness in things that don't matter.

The people of Thailand did the same thing. This golden statue was covered in plaster and clay for over a century, ignored, and left out in the elements. It was only when the cheap covering cracked, exposing the masterpiece within, that the statue's true worth was realized.

I came across a statistic a few years ago that shook me. I haven't been able to forget it. A recent Gallup poll found that 70% of people hate their job. That means about three out of four people absolutely hate what they do for a living. I don't mean a kind of hate resulting from long hours and needing a vacation. I mean they hate their job with an intensity that requires them to numb their senses in order to make it through the workweek. Speaker and author Jon Acuff says, "Anything you do for 40 to 60 hours a week for 40 to 60 years, is your life." I don't want my kids to grow up hating their life. I want them to grow up living and loving every minute of their life!

Life is too precious and short to spend it squeaking out a safe existence covered in cheap plaster. We all have a gift given inside of us. God has given each of us a unique gift and talent. And until we live each day using these gifts and talents to bring glory to God, we'll continue to add layers of protection, hoping to fit in among others who are hiding their true identities from the world. We've long forgotten about God's gift inside us and are only concerned with hiding our true identity.

We don't want our children to grow up feeling they need to cover and hide their God-given identity. We want them to know they're loved, made in the image of God, and more valuable than they could ever imagine. We want them to be confident, using their gifts and talents to bring glory to God.

YOUR LOVE AND APPROVAL

Just like the monk looking under the covering, we must always shine a light on the gift that God has placed in us and our children helping them chip away the cheap covering the world places on them. When our children have our love and approval, they will live with the confidence to chase after all their dreams and desires.

Kids struggle to fit in. The world conditions our kids to ignore their God-given identity and settle for mediocrity.

The result is our kids add layers of protection around their hearts and minds, believing they're a cheap clay statue and not a priceless gift of God. They grow up afraid to reveal their true identity. As parents, we need to remind our kids that they're created in the image of God. They are his masterpiece, designed to do good works. When the world tries to cover them with cheap coverings, we need to remind them of their God-given value. Kids will always look to their parents first when the world tries to force them to cover up and fit in. Believe me, you can do more to encourage your child than even their closest friends.

As parents, we need to help our kids identify the gifts God has given them. My oldest son Ethan is a gifted storyteller who loves to communicate. Maddie has a loving, mothering spirit. Charlie is light-hearted, fun, and filled with kindness.

If I try to make Charlie have a mothering spirit like Maddie, I would cause him to doubt his God-given identity. He would begin to add layers of protection over his heart, mind, and soul. He would feel he needed to earn my love and approval. If I forced Maddie to love communication like Ethan, she could feel pressured to enter a field of study revolving around communication so she could earn my love and approval. If I were to make Ethan tweak his personality to be more light-hearted like Charlie, he would feel pressured to live up to my expectations so he could earn my love and approval.

Helping your kids discover their God-given gifts and talents is a journey. Here are some questions to help someone begin to identify their gifts and talents.

- What are three things you are naturally good at?
- What comes easy to you?
- What do others compliment you on?
- What gets you in trouble? (I know this may seem strange, but some gifts and talents are uncovered in times of trouble. For instance, Charlie loves to tell jokes and entertain. It doesn't always work well in his classes, but given the right profession, it will work well for him as an adult.)
- What challenges or hardships have you overcome?
- What brings you joy?
- What skills have you developed?
- What special knowledge or education have you acquired?
- Who or what inspires you? Why?
- What makes you cry? Smile? Laugh? Angry? Why?

These questions will hopefully help you begin to crack the casing to discover your child's God-given talents. There's space at the end of this chapter for you to brainstorm answers for each question.

As parents, when we focus on the good stuff like giving our kids our love and approval, we set them up for a lifetime of success as they embrace their God-given identity. They'll believe and know they're loved by God and more valuable than any statue, even a solid gold statue as valuable as the Golden Buddha. When your child realizes their God-given value, they'll never again be satisfied with the world's cheap coverings.

Never make your kids earn your love and approval. Build them up. Help them identify their God-given identity.

Life is fun when you focus on giving your kids the good stuff like your love and approval.

More Good Stuff
The story in the next chapter provided one of the greatest parenting strategies ever implemented in the Poland home! The change was positive, instant, and long lasting. It can do the same for your family.

Reflect on the Good Stuff

Let's crack the casing on your child's God-given identity.

1. What are three things you're naturally good at?

2. What comes easy to you?

3. What do others compliment you on?

4. What gets you in trouble?

5. What challenges have you overcome?

6. What brings you joy?

7. What skills have you developed?

8. What special knowledge or education have you acquired?

9. Who or what inspires you? Why?

10. What makes you cry? Smile? Laugh? Angry? Why?

CHAPTER 2

Reward Your Kids

*Look, I am coming soon! My reward is with
me, and I will give to each person according to
what they have done.* —Revelation 22:12 (NIV)

The day started out like any other winter day: cold,
damp, and grey. The kids and I headed out the door to
school. After dropping them off, I made my way to the
local tire shop for four new tires. I mean, who doesn't
love dropping a fortune on rubber.

After a quick conversation with the sales clerk, I hand
him my keys and make my way to the coffee pot. I pour a
cup of coffee, nod hello to the other patrons and sit down
for a nice peaceful morning doing the crossword puzzle
in the newspaper as I wait for my vehicle to get new tires.

Within moments of sitting down, the door swings open.
In walks a mom lugging an infant in a car seat along with
two toddlers in tow. These kiddos are adorable. The mom
makes her way to the service counter. After a brief
conversation with the sales clerk, she drags herself to the
waiting area and sits down, placing the baby beside her

on the floor in his car seat with the two young kids by her side. Since these two kids aren't in school, I assume they're 4 or 5 years old. The patrons in the tire shop smile at the mom and her children. Such a beautiful young family!

The beauty quickly fades as the two toddlers leap from their chairs and begin roaming around the tire shop. What happens next is truly unbelievable!

These two kids begin to dismantle everything! They climb on the tire and rim displays. They push all the buttons on the soda machine. They turn the knobs on the candy machines. They spit on the windows. They lick the windows! Yes! They lick the windows! They run and scream throughout the building. This behavior continues for a good half hour.

The entire time these two kids are destroying the tire shop, their mother is on her cell phone, talking to a friend. She repeatedly barks at the kids, saying, "I can't wait for your daddy to get here! Whenever your daddy gets here, you're going to get in trouble!" These threats don't faze the kids. They continue running and screaming, climbing on everything, and spitting on and licking the windows.

At this point, the infant in the car seat chimes in with a cough. Not a small cough like a baby who chokes on his milk but that deep, raspy, lung-strangling respiratory cough infants get during the wintertime. His mom, to everyone's surprise, does absolutely nothing to help her baby stop coughing. She remains on her phone, talking with her friend and yelling at the other two kids, "I can't wait for your daddy to get here!"

I'm reminded of Charlton Heston's line from *Planet of the Apes*. "IT'S A MADHOUSE! A MADHOUSE!"

The baby coughs for what seems like an eternity. The patrons in the tire shop are looking at each other as if to say, "If she doesn't do something quickly, we're going to help this sweet baby breathe!" Directly, the mom takes the infant out the car seat and begins to pat him on the back. She's not overly concerned about this cough because she remains on the phone.

While patting the baby on the back, she tells her friend on the phone, "Girl, I'm just sitting here watching my friend's baby, and he's got a terrible cough."

Those of us in the tire shop look at each other in amazement. This small sweet precious baby, this gift of God, is not her child! Some unsuspecting mom and dad trusted this lady to watch their precious newborn. It's obvious to everyone that she's more concerned about her phone conversation with her friend than with the well-being of this little baby. This isn't her child! We can't believe it!

The chaos continues until the door to the tire shop swings open. In walks Daddy. He corrals the kids and marches them outside to his vehicle. The mom follows him, holding the coughing infant. Judging from the expressive conversation between the mom and dad, as witnessed by everyone through the spit-covered windows, she's dogging him out for their kids' behavior. I have no idea what she's saying but it's very clear that she's relaying her dissatisfaction to her husband. The patrons in the store look around at each another in bewilderment. We don't know what to say or do. It's such a strange set of circumstances.

The clerk at the counter lets me know that my vehicle is ready. I pay for the tires and tell him that I hope the rest of his day is less eventful! He smiles and says, "Yeah, me too!"

Later that afternoon, I picked up my kids from school. Without telling them my plans, we head to the local Walmart. My kids recognized we weren't going home and asked where we were going. During the short drive to Walmart, I told them the story of the morning's events at the tire shop, how the two young kids climbed on, spit on, and jumped on everything in the tire shop. Their eyes got big as saucers. They couldn't believe kids would behave this way. They still had no idea why we were heading to Walmart.

I told them the reason we were going to Walmart was because they were being rewarded for not treating their parents the way the two kids from the tire shop treated their parents. There was plenty of blame for the parents, but it was obvious those two disobedient children didn't listen to their mom or dad.

Then I dropped the bombshell. "Your mom and dad want to show you how much we appreciate you for not treating us like those two kids. When we get to Walmart, you can have ANYTHING you want!"

The kids looked at me and asked, "Anything?"

"That's right, ANYTHING! It's our reward to you for being well behaved and not treating your parents the way those kids treated their parents."

At Walmart, I turned to Ethan to see what he wanted. Ethan, who had a preteen bottomless pit of a stomach, was hungry and wanted a snack from McDonald's. We ordered a quarter-pounder, fries, and a soda.

Then I turned to Maddie and Charlie. Maddie was 7. Charlie was 5. I knew what they would say, but I asked them anyway. They asked again to make sure they had heard me correctly, "We can have anything we want?"

"That's correct! You can have ANYTHING you want."

You guessed it! We were heading to the toy aisle. Maddie and Charlie looked at the toys on every aisle before making their decision. Maddie chose a doll. Charlie chose an action figure.

The entire trip to Walmart cost me less than $25. Ethan's food was $5. Maddie's doll was $9. Charlie's action figure was $8.

REWARD YOUR KIDS

Rewards. Some people love to give them while others hate to give them. One thing is certain; we all love to get them! We love to know our actions are being noticed. When a parent, boss, teacher, anyone really, recognizes and acknowledges our actions, we stand a little taller and are filled with pride. Not a dangerous type of pride that leads to destruction, but pride that builds a person's self-esteem.

Rewards can play a crucial part in the emotional well-being of your child. When you as a parent rewards your child for behavior you value, your child views this as a win. They clearly know your expectations and realize they've risen to meet these expectations. Your child is happier and the bond between you and your child is strengthened.

The tire shop is a story of how we effectively use rewards in our home to raise confident, healthy, and happy children. We reward behavior we value.

The tire shop parable cost less than $25 but provided a teachable moment that has lived on in our family. It taught our kids more about their parents' expectations than any sit-down lecture or book ever could. In our home, we reward behavior we value.

Rewards conjure up mixed emotions among parents. My wife and I always look for opportunities to reward our kids. We don't have a set system in place. We don't use a reward chart. We simply reward behavior we value, such as hard work, generosity, caring for others, and loving the unlovable, just to name a few.

Rewards are biblical

If you struggle with rewarding your children, let me remind you that rewards are biblical. The Bible makes it very clear that our behavior on Earth is directly tied to our eternal rewards.

> In Galatians 6:9 (NIV), Paul tells us, *"Let us not become weary in doing good, for at the proper time we will reap a harvest if we do not give up."*

> In Matthew 7:11 (NIV), Jesus says, *"If you, then, though you are evil, know how to give good gifts to your children, how much more will your Father in heaven give good gifts to those who ask him!"*

> Jesus says in Revelation 22:12 (NIV), *"Look, I am coming soon! My reward is with me, and I will give to each person according to what they have done."*

We know these verses aren't talking about the reward of salvation. Ephesians 2:8-9 makes it plain that we're saved by grace through faith. Salvation is not based on our actions or behavior. It's based on the finished work of Christ. The rewards we'll enjoy throughout eternity are directly tied to our actions here on Earth. God rewards behavior he values. That's a pretty good example to follow!

Rewards motivate

The key to using rewards as a motivator is your focus. You must focus on the behavior you value not the reward itself. Focusing on the reward rather than the behavior will have a negative effect. When the reward is the goal, people are willing to do whatever necessary to earn the reward.

In his book *Drive*, Daniel Pink says, "The problem with making an extrinsic reward the only destination that matters is that some people will choose the quickest route there, even if it means taking the low road. Indeed, most of the scandals and misbehavior that have seemed endemic to modern life involve shortcuts."

Rewarding behavior you value will motivate your child to do more of this behavior. Rewarding our kids on a regular basis has helped solve almost every discipline issue we've faced as parents. I know it can do the same for you.

Rewards build your child's self-esteem

A May 2014 article on the CDC (Centers for Disease Control) website states, "When a child earns a reward, he knows he has done something good and something you like." Many kids have low self-esteem because they feel like a failure. They don't think they can do anything right.

When you reward small victories, your child's confidence increases. When their confidence increases, so does their self-esteem.

Rewards strengthen your relationship

When you give your child a reward, it makes them happy. They go to school happy. Their friends will notice they're happy. Don't misunderstand me. I'm not suggesting you spend your days dreaming up ways to make your child happy. Kids who think the world revolves around them become spoiled brats. Don't raise a house full of Nellie Olesons or Veruca Salts! As a parent, I look for opportunities to reward my kids for behavior I value. A byproduct of consistent rewards is a happy child. Obedience breeds happiness.

On a recent field trip with my oldest son Ethan, as class stopped for lunch, I began talking with a couple of my son's classmates. One of them commented, "I admire how much you love your kids. It really shows. You're always willing to do things with your child and for your child. I think you're an awesome parent."

This was a teenager! A teenage girl at that! You know, one of those kids that everyone says are so terrible and only concerned with themselves and their phone. This sweet young lady realized I have a strong connection with my teenage son.

Notice what she didn't say. She did not say, "I know you love your kids because you buy them gifts." Nor did she say, "Your kids love you because you buy them gifts." She realized that I have a great relationship with my high school senior, a teenager. One of the ways I have strengthened this relationship through the years is by rewarding behavior that I value.

Before I share some of the rewards we use with our kids, let me give you six reward disclaimers.

Reward Disclaimer #1
We don't reward minimal behavior that must be done as part of our family. We're a family and expect everyone to pitch in. We expect our children to help do the dishes, the laundry, clean the yard, etc. These minimal behaviors and actions are expected and are not rewarded.

Reward Disclaimer #2
We don't give our children an allowance. In his podcast, Dave Ramsey once said he didn't give his kids an allowance because no one gives you money for free. In life, money is given as payment for work. We do, from time to time, give our children spending money simply because we love them but not as a regular allowance.

Reward Disclaimer #3
We never reward our children when they ask, "Will I get something if I do this?" We don't want to teach our children that every action will be rewarded. Someone who acts only when rewarded is selfish. We don't encourage this behavior.

Reward Disclaimer #4
A reward is not a bribe. As my good friend, Jim Wideman says, "A bribe is payment for an illegal act." A reward is something given based on performance.

Reward Disclaimer #5
Rewards are not "everyone gets a trophy." Everyone wins is a terrible parenting model. If one child earns a reward, then reward only that child. Their brothers and sisters do not get rewarded.

Reward Disclaimer #6
If you miss a reward, it's okay! Don't beat yourself up. Tell your child you're sorry and you owe them one. They'll forgive you. You don't have to follow your child around with pen and paper. Let the rewards flow out of your normal daily life. If, after the fact, you learn your child has done something amazing, reward them then!

Behaviors We Reward

Going above and beyond
This is a reward given when our kids go above and beyond what's expected of them without being asked. When our kids take the initiative to clean the fridge, organize the pantry, clean the bathrooms, etc., we reward them.

Doing something good for someone else
We love to reward our kids when they put others first. This shows us they realize the world doesn't revolve

around them. Anytime they're willing to do something good for someone else, we make it a big deal!

Report cards
It's nothing new to reward good grades. However, we also reward our kids when they work hard to make an improvement in a subject in which they're struggling. We don't demand all A's, but we do demand an A effort. If they work hard to improve their grades, we'll reward their diligence.

Not *acting a fool* at the doctor's office
This is an area we rewarded when our kids were younger. Kids often pitch a fit just walking into the doctor's office. We didn't want our kids to *act a fool*, so we rewarded good behavior at the doctor's office.

Just because we love you
We never want our children to feel like they must earn our love or approval. That's why, from time to time, we simply buy them gifts just because we love them. To some, it may look like we spoil our kids. I'm okay with that! I've heard a lot of people pray and ask God to "bless them" or "bless their family." I want to model a loving and generous Heavenly Father. If you're struggling with this type of reward, I encourage you to read what the Bible says about rewards. God loves to reward his children for behavior he values.

Completing a difficult task or project
It's true that kid problems aren't on the same level as adult problems. However, kids face their own difficulties.

Anytime our children complete a difficult task, assignment, or project, we want to reward their hard work.

I can't believe how awesome you are!

For this reward, remember the tire shop parable. We want our kids to know any behavior like that of the two young kids in the tire shop is unacceptable. I could have made my point by having a family meeting. But show is better than tell. We love teachable moments. The incident in the tire shop provided the perfect teachable moment to spotlight behavior we value.

Rewards our kids love

I know what you're thinking, *This sounds expensive! There is no way I can afford to reward my kids every time their actions or behavior line up with my values.* I understand that. We don't reward everything all the time. We don't chart it. When we notice behavior we value, we reward it. Even if it's simply words of affirmation. Remember, the trip to Walmart cost less than $25 total for my three kids. This $25 has paid itself back a thousand times over.

The following are examples of rewards we give our children. These aren't set in stone. The cost of each will vary. None will break the bank.

Choose a meal

When you allow a child to choose what or where the family will eat, it's huge. Most children spend every day being told what to do by every adult in their life. When a child is allowed to make a decision on the choice of something as simple as a meal, it's empowering. It doesn't have to be the choice of restaurant. It can simply be allowing your child to choose what you will cook at home. Remember choice is power.

Checkout counter goodies

We don't do this every time but, from time to time, we will allow our kids to pick something from the goodies located at the checkout counter. Remember you're rewarding behavior you value; so if you're in the checkout line and your child has a meltdown, don't reward this behavior. You'll do more harm than good.

Take them (and their friends) to lunch

This reward has multiple benefits. A couple times each school year, we check each of our kids out of school and take them to lunch. They love it! Especially our teenager! If you want to take this reward to the next level, allow them to invite a classmate. Contact their parents ahead of time to get permission of course. Your child will love you. Their friend will love your child. Your child's friend will love you. The parents of your child's friend will love you and your child! Everyone wins.

You can have ANYTHING you want

Save this reward for those *I cannot believe how awesome you are* moments. We've only used this a couple times in all our years of parenting. It has never costs more than $25 combined for all three children.

A word of warning! If you've never rewarded your child, this is not the place to start. If you do start here, plan to spend a lot of money. But because we reward behavior we value on a regular basis, this reward doesn't cost us an arm and a leg.

Final Thoughts on Rewards

Start Early

Start rewarding behavior you value as early as possible. The sooner you implement rewards in your home, the better. However, if you have a teenager in your home whom you've seldom, if ever, rewarded, it's not too late to begin rewarding the behavior you value.

Go to your teenager and say, "I just want to let you know I love you. Let's go get some ice cream because I think you're wonderful." Be ready for blank stares!

Or try something like this, "You know I've been reminded today of how much I love you. Is there something special I can cook you for supper that would let you know how much I love you?" The simple things really do make a difference.

Take the Jesus Approach

Recall Revelation 22:12 (NIV), "Look, I am coming soon! My reward is with me, and I will give to each person according to what they have done."

God is a loving and generous Heavenly Father. He gave us the greatest reward in his Son, Jesus. Jesus encourages us that when he returns, he's not coming empty handed. He'll be bringing rewards to give to each of us for the behavior and actions that He values. You can do the same!

Rewards are the good stuff. Reward behavior you value. Find something over the next couple days you value and reward your kids. It doesn't have to cost you any money. A simple "I love you" or "Thank you" will go a long way.

More Good Stuff

What do you do if you've given your love and approval, faithfully rewarded behavior you value, only to have your kids come up short? It's time to talk about the fun topic of failure.

Reflect on the Good Stuff

1. What behaviors do you value?

2. Of the behaviors listed in this chapter, which will you begin to reward?

3. Which of the rewards will you begin to use with your kids?

CHAPTER 3

Failure

Failure is a bruise not a tattoo. —Jon Sinclair

Success is the ability to go from one failure to the next without the loss of enthusiasm.
—Winston Churchill

Failure is the opportunity to begin again more intelligently. —Henry Ford

One hot Louisiana summer day my phone rang. It was my mother calling to tell me she had purchased an above-ground swimming pool on clearance at Walmart. There was nothing wrong with this pool. It was on clearance, and she bought it at a ridiculously cheap price. She was so excited that her grandson Ethan would have a pool at his house.

This pool wasn't one of those giant inflatable pools, held in place by water. This was a sturdy above-ground pool with metal walls and pool liner. My mother knew I would be able to build the pool because I was a civil engineer. Civil engineers design structures for a living. There was no question in her mind that I would be able to build a simple above-ground swimming pool.

Ethan and I promptly picked out the perfect spot for the pool. This new pool would look great just off the deck in our backyard. We used our deck to entertain friends. A pool would provide many memories for family and friends. Once the pool was operational, Ethan and I could extend the deck around the pool. Perfect!

Before we could install the pool, we had to level the ground. Our house was built on a hill with the backyard sloped away from the house. This meant we would need to level off a hill. We didn't care. We were going to have our own swimming pool.

We got to work. The only equipment we had available was a couple of shovels. It took an entire weekend to remove all the vegetation, dig into the hill, and level the foundation for the pool. And just to be clear, we didn't build this pool in the middle of spring or fall. It was the height of a hot Louisiana summer. No shade trees. No cool breezes. Just sweat-inducing heat and humidity. We didn't mind the hard work because we knew this pool would provide hours of enjoyment for our family and friends. We could already envision lounging on the deck, barbecuing, and swimming.

This was going to be fantastic!

The pool was 24 feet in diameter. The installation appeared to be straightforward. Metal walls supported by braces every five feet around the perimeter. A rubber pool liner formed the bottom. This next part is embarrassing to admit. Maybe because I'm a civil engineer. Maybe because I'm a man and we struggle admitting our mistakes. Or maybe it's a combination of many things and I just took for granted the project ahead of me. Regardless, after getting the ground level, I discarded the instructions. And by discarded, I don't mean I misplaced them. I don't mean I accidentally lost them or placed them to the side. I mean I intentionally threw them in the trash.

Who needs instructions? Not this guy! I'm a grown man and a civil engineer I don't need a set of instructions to build a simple above-ground swimming pool.

Mistake.

With the foundation in place, Ethan and I began constructing the swimming pool. The first step was to install the metal walls. The walls were constructed of thin sheets of metal not much thicker than a piece of paper. Yet, when formed in a circle and held in place by the pool water, they were sure to be extremely strong.

With the pool wall in place, we installed the liner stretching it up to and over the top of the walls. The liner was temporarily clipped to the top of the walls using wooden clothespins. For those not raised in the country, clothes pins are small wooden clips used to hold wet clothing on to outside wire or rope called a clothesline.

The ground was level. The pool walls were up. The liner was stretched and in place. Looking around, I noticed several pieces left uninstalled. The supporting brackets for the walls were supposed to be installed around the perimeter of the pool. The engineer and the man in me decided that we could leave the braces out. I mean the pressure from the water would be more than enough to keep the walls vertical. I put those braces in the same pile as the instructions.

Ethan and I began to fill the swimming pool with water. Each afternoon, Ethan asked the same question, "Dad! Is the pool ready?"

"No, son, the pool isn't quite ready. But when it's ready, it's going to be so awesome! I can't wait to go swimming in our own pool." We would walk around the pool each afternoon inspecting the walls and liner to make certain it was filling properly. We inspected the clothespins.

The second afternoon, Ethan asked the same question, "Dad, is the pool ready?"

"We're getting close, but it's not quite ready. It won't be long now. Pretty soon, we'll be enjoying the fruits of our labor. Let's go check everything!"

You know how the Bible says, "On the third day..."? Well, on the third day, Ethan asked his question one more time. "Dad, is the pool ready?"

We walked outside for our daily inspection. A giant smile came to my face. "Son, today is the day you've been waiting for. The pool is ready!"

The joy on my son's face was worth all the hot, sweaty, back-breaking work put in over the last several weekends. I was one proud papa!

"All we need to do at this point, Son, is remove the clothespins and secure the liner in place. That should only take a few minutes."

"Can I play in the pool while you secure the liner?"

"I don't see why not. Why don't you wear your pool floatie until I can get in the pool with you?"

"Awesome! It's already inflated and ready to go!"

We walked out onto our deck overlooking our backyard. Now remember, our house was built on the hill, so our backyard slopes down and away from our house. We walked to the end of our deck and smiled at the beautiful pool. We could envision how wonderful the expanded deck would look around the pool. Neither of us had to say what we were feeling, "This swimming pool is going to provide years of enjoyment for our family!"

Ethan asked, "Can I jump in?"

"I think you'll be fine. You can play in the pool and I'll get busy securing the liner."

Ethan, with his pool floatie around his waist, jumped off the deck railing into the pool. "Woohoo! This is so awesome! Thanks, Dad! I know it was hard work, but it was worth it!"

I smiled as Ethan bounced and played in the swimming pool. He was barely tall enough to touch the bottom and keep his head above water. But with the help of the floatie, he was safe.

The sun was shining. Not a cloud in the sky. Another beautiful hot, sweaty Louisiana afternoon. We were so excited.

As Ethan was playing in the pool, I made my way around the swimming pool, securing the pool liner.

While securing the pool liner, I heard thunder. This is Louisiana. Afternoon thundershowers aren't unusual. In fact, many times, thundershowers can appear out of nowhere, rain for a few minutes, and then disappear as quickly as they appeared. I thought nothing of the thunder and continued securing the pool liner.

The thunder came again. This time with a little more intensity. A quick glance in the sky. Again, no clouds. As I brought my head back down, I noticed Ethan bouncing in the pool water. He was jumping up and down screaming and hollering. He was having a ball. That's when I noticed the pool liner. The top few inches of the pool liner yet to be secured had fallen and were now floating on top of the water. As Ethan jumped up and down, water would squirt in between the pool liner and the pool walls. At this point, I realized what was happening.

It wasn't thunder I was hearing. It was the sound of the metal walls vibrating. I knew the pool was about to collapse. I had to get Ethan out immediately! This next part happened so fast yet has replayed so slow in my mind for years.

The walls vibrated violently one final time and it was as if someone stuck their arm into the center of the pool liner and turned it inside out. You know how people say in the blink of an eye, something happens? Well, in the blink of an eye, all 10,000 gallons of pool water came gushing out, sending Ethan surfing down the backyard on his pool floatie.

One moment, Ethan was bouncing in the pool. The next moment he was gone! Imagine being in the middle of a giant untied balloon filled with water surfing down a hill. Before I could even think, Ethan was almost a football field in length away from me.

My mind was a whirlwind of emotions. Was Ethan okay? When the pool collapsed, he surfed out under the metal pool walls. Had the walls sliced him in half like a ninja? Would Ethan be in two pieces at the bottom of the hill?

Coming to my senses, I ran to the bottom of the hill to check on Ethan. "Son, son, are you okay? Are you okay? Speak to me!"

When I reached Ethan, I quickly looked him over head to toe. Not a single scratch, no blood, no bruises. His facial expression said it all: "Can we do that again!"

"Do that again? Are you insane!? No, we can't do that again! All our hard work just went down this hill with you and your floatie!"

We climbed back up the hill, dragging the shredded pool liner and my dignity behind us. As we surveyed the damage, it was evident the pool was a complete disaster. The metal walls had crumbled together like a piece of tinfoil taken off the Christmas pie. Every piece was bent, mangled, and shredded beyond repair. A total loss.

FAILURE

Now I know you're thinking, *This sounds like a pretty cool story.* But I promise you, at that moment, I felt like the biggest failure as a father. I let my son down. The pool collapse could have severely injured him. I'm thankful to God that Ethan wasn't injured because of my stupidity. For years, every time I looked at a swimming pool, I was reminded of my failure. Each time we used our deck, the circular cutout into the hill from the missing pool served as a visual reminder of my biggest failure as a dad.

There are few things in life as devastating as failure. I don't know anyone who likes to fail.

This story of the pool recounts the time I felt like the biggest failure as a father. It's the story of failure due to several bad choices I made over a relatively short time. While I didn't find this story humorous at the time, looking back, there were several funny moments. When I tell this story to live audiences, they laugh uncontrollably. Trust me, at the time, I was not thrilled! There was no joy, no excitement, and laughter was the furthest thing from my mind.

My wife has often said that one of my best qualities is believing the best about people. I believe the overwhelming majority of people want to do the right thing. We may struggle with the application or implementation, but I believe most people, when given the choice, will do what's right. Yet, even the best of intentions can lead to failure.

We're human and we do fail. Most failures can be placed in two categories. One category is a failure due to our choices. Even though we want to do the right thing, many times, we just don't and our choices cause us to fail. These failures, whether public or private, can do damage to our spirit and ego.

The second category of failure is coming up short. We practice. We give maximum effort. But at the end of the day, we just come up short. Whether in a sporting contest, an assignment at work, or another avenue in life, we simply come up short. I've learned not to view this experience as failure. The world may view this as a failure, but I do not.

Author and leadership guru, John Maxwell, says, "Sometimes we win and sometimes we learn." We need to realize that we won't succeed at everything we put our hand to. There will be difficulties at times in life and, in many of those times, we'll simply come up short. We need to begin to view failure as part of the learning process.

We all have experienced failure in our life. I have certainly had my fair share. I've done things I'm terribly ashamed of. It took me a long time to get comfortable telling this story to more than my closest friends because of the embarrassment I felt. I realize failure doesn't define you as a person. As Zig Ziglar used to say, "Failure is an event. Not a person." I failed building a swimming pool. I wasn't a failure as a father.

I know this may seem strange to consider failure as part of the good stuff in our lives, so let me explain. We need to help our kids understand that failure is part of life. We need to help them learn from their failures. They won't succeed every time they try something new. They'll be laughed at, picked on, and overlooked. I'm not suggesting that you teach them to live accepting failure and abuse as normal, but I am suggesting you help them understand failure is a natural part of life.

A proper understanding of failure is vital for them becoming functioning adults. Too many folks believe successful people are only successful because they cheated, lied, and stepped on the necks of others on their way to the top. They fail to realize that successful people experience failure too. Successful people just don't let it stop them or hold them back. Winston Churchill says, "Success is the ability to go from one failure to the next without the loss of enthusiasm." Properly understanding failure is a key to success.

Here's a list of some famous failures to consider. Walt Disney was fired because his employer said he had no imagination. Steven Spielberg was rejected from three film schools. The first school that rejected him now has a building named after him. Albert Einstein couldn't speak until the age of four. Abraham Lincoln lost eight elections before becoming president.

How you respond to your failures will determine how your child handles their failures. If you try to cover them up, your child will do the same. If you complain and blame other for your failures, your child will do the same. If you embrace failure as part of life, seeking to learn from your failures, your child will do the same.

This is how we handle failures of choice in our home. First, we admit our mistakes. We admit that our choices lead to the consequences we are experiencing. Next, we address the issue. With our children, we give consequences that fit the offense. Lastly, we move on. Unless the actions continue, we don't bring it up again. Nor do we look for opportunities to remind our kids of their mistakes. The Bible says in Micah 7:19 that God buries our sins in the sea of forgetfulness. This is good advice that many parents need to put into practice. Admit it. Address it. Move on!

Now, if your child has failed by coming up short, I want to encourage you to begin to view this as a learning experience and not a failure. Jon Sinclair says, "Failure is a bruise not a tattoo." The only time coming up short becomes failure is if your child quits trying to improve. Encourage them to try again. If it's a hobby, a failure can be a good time to evaluate. Is this an area they really enjoy? Are they really gifted in this area? Is this something you're pushing on them? Turn their failures into learning opportunities. Remember the words of Henry Ford: "Failure is the opportunity to begin again more intelligently."

As your kids go through life, they'll experience failure. Help them succeed by embracing and learning from their failures. Embracing failure is key to a fun life!

A final thought regarding the pool story, unless you plan on sharing your failures with masses of people, it's much cheaper and safer to use the public pool!

More Good Stuff
Now that we know how to properly handle failure, let's talk about four extraordinary habits that will catapult your kids lightyears ahead of their peers.

Reflect on the Good Stuff

1. What failures have you or your children experienced?

2. How did you respond to these failures?

3. What did you and your child learn from these failures?

4. How did you help your child learn from their failures?

CHAPTER 4

Extraordinary Habits

It's easier to prevent bad habits than break them. —Ben Franklin

A habit cannot be tossed out the window. It must be coaxed down the stairs one step at a time. —Mark Twain

Who's the one family member that everyone loves? Who's the one family member, that if they were missing, your family would not be the same? Who comes to mind?

For me, it's easy. Mamaw Lizzie. For those outside the South, *Mamaw* is a term of endearment for our grandmothers. It's a much less formal greeting than grandmother but it carries the same level of respect, love, and admiration.

Mamaw Lizzie is a very special person. When I was a newborn, my mother would wake me up long before daylight, get me dressed, and take me to Mamaw Lizzie's house. My mother's work schedule allowed me to spend a lot of quality time with Mamaw Lizzie. I'm certain this is one reason we continue to have a special bond. At the time of this writing, Mamaw Lizzie is a beautiful 94 years old.

I spent a lot of my childhood with Mamaw Lizzie. I would spend as much of my summer breaks with her as allowed. I have so many great childhood memories from my time with her. Her house didn't have the latest gadgets and gizmos. It was your typical grandmother's home. Very simple. Always clean. Pictures of kids and grandkids covering the walls. The living room housed one very prized possession. A giant white tail deer she killed in 1969, a massive 13-point buck that held the record as the largest deer killed by a woman in the state of Arkansas for 30 years, earning her the title "Arkansas's First Lady of Deer Hunting." But that's another story for another book.

Our favorite game to play during the day was Solitaire. Mamaw would encourage me to "Get out the cards and see if you can beat ole Sol!" I spent hours on end at her kitchen table playing Solitaire while Mamaw Lizzie drank her tea and watched her soaps. These are some of my favorite childhood memories.

Of the many things I remember about Mamaw Lizzie's house was the hallway outside her bathroom. At some point, a water pipe had burst under the house causing water to flood the subfloor. The result was a massive bubble in the linoleum flooring that remained permanently damaged. Through the years, the bubble had torn, creating a tripping hazard as you walked down the hall.

I never quite understood why the damage section wasn't removed and properly repaired. The damaged flooring remained a fixture in the home until she sold her home and moved in with my parents.

Mamaw Lizzie did do one thing to keep everyone from tripping over the torn linoleum. She covered the damaged area with a rug. When the edges of the linoleum would curl and harden, she would take the rug off, trim the linoleum, and lay the rug back down. When she cleaned her house, she would remove the rug, sweep out the dirt, and place the rug back over the damaged area. Because this subfloor was never properly repaired, the floor always caused a tripping hazard. This rug was Mamaw's way of covering up the dangerous tripping hazard in her home.

EXTRAORDINARY HABITS

Just as Mamaw Lizzie's flooring was a dangerous tripping hazard, we have another kind of tripping hazard in our lives: bad habits. We all have bad habits in our lives that trip us up. We often go to elaborate measures to cover up and hide our bad habits. We buy expensive coverings, hoping those closest to us will never notice. On occasion, we may even uncover our bad habits and attempt to clean them up.

What's your rug hiding? What have you covered up in the hope that it will disappear? What do you wish you'd never started that's become part of your normal life? Emotional shopping? Secrets? A terrible relationship? Overmedicating? Spending too much time online? Breaking promises? Being unfriendly? Avoiding or skipping work? Yelling? Complaining? Losing your temper?

We all have bad habits in our lives that we wished we never started in first place. We've become so comfortable with them that they're now a normal part of our lives. Rather than work to overcome them, we cover them up with smiles, secrets, and excuses, hoping no one finds out the ugly truth. Just like the rug in Mamaw Lizzie's house, the rug hides the ugly truth of our bad habits.

I'm not sure what your rug is hiding, but I'm certain you know. What comes to mind?

As parents, we need to help our kids develop extraordinary habits. We need to help them identify areas in their life they're covering up and ignoring. We need to help them develop better habits.

Through the years, I've had the privilege of working with kids and families from all walks of life. On the outside, we all look perfectly fine. But when pressed to be open and honest, almost every family will admit they struggle with the consequences of their bad habits. The struggles vary from family to family, but every family struggles. If you think your family is the only one that struggles, you're sadly mistaken.

It would be impossible to create an exhaustive list of extraordinary habits. However, these four extraordinary habits are four that we help our kids develop and practice regularly because we believe they provide a foundation for many other great habits to build upon. Modeling these habits for your kids will help them develop these habits as a natural part of their lives. Remember show is better than tell.

Extraordinary Habit #1 – Patience

There's a line in the movie *Evan Almighty* that's not a direct Bible verse but certainly lines up with good theology. *Evan Almighty* is a very loose modern tale of the story of Noah. It's not intended to be even remotely accurate to the biblical account. Really the only true biblical parallels are that there is a man who is married with three kids who is asked to build a boat, gather animals and of course a flood. But the flood in *Evan Almighty* is very small. Nothing compared to the Biblical flood.

Evan, played by Steve Carrell, is asked to build a boat by God, played by Morgan Freeman. Evan has no desire to build the Ark until he realizes he cannot escape God's plan. He reluctantly begins to assemble the Ark, creating a source of tension and frustration within his family. At one point, his wife has had enough and leaves with their three boys. While they're traveling, they stop in a diner for lunch. Morgan Freeman comes to her secretly disguised as a waiter working in the diner. Realizing she's worried and stressed, he strikes up a conversation. That's when the scene occurs.

Morgan Freeman says, and this is a paraphrase, "If someone prays for patience, do you think God just zaps them patience or does he give them the opportunity to be patient? If someone prays for their family to be closer, do you think God just zaps them with warm fuzzy feelings or does he give them the opportunity to love one another?"

I love that exchange! Too often, we pray for God to zap us with patience. But that's not how it works. When we pray for patience, God doesn't zap us with superhero levels of patience. He gives us the opportunity to be patient. Let's be honest, as parents, we have many, many opportunities to be patient.

Patience is one thing I prayed for when I became a new Christian. I came to Christ at the age of 25 and quickly realized I needed patience. I told some of my fellow brothers and sisters in Christ that I was praying for patience. They always grunted and said, "Pray for anything but don't pray for patience!"

The first six months of praying for patience was torture. God gave me many, many opportunities to be patient. But the great thing is we've been able to pass this extraordinary habit along to our children. Our kids aren't perfect but they do have parents who model patience for them. They do a great job of modeling patience at a young age.

We live in a world of instant everything. Anything you could want is at our fingertips. If you want food, order and it will be delivered to your house. In some cities, you can even order your meals directly from your smartphone without having to speak to a live human being. Want to watch a movie, download it on a tablet, smartphone, or TV. Need to talk to a friend? You have text, email, Facebook, Twitter, Messenger, Instagram, Snapchat, or whatever new cool social media platform is available these days. Everything is instant.

Life isn't instant. Some things take time. Learning a new skill takes time. Learning to play the piano takes time. Education takes time. Relationships take time. Learning to be patient takes time. God won't zap you or your kids with loads of patience. You will have to develop this extraordinary habit by practicing patience every day.

Extraordinary Habit #2 – Boundaries
I read a study where scientists experimented with the fence around a school playground. The scientists observed the children running and playing over the entirety of the playground. The children utilized all the playground equipment playing on all the grassy areas within the fenced-in playground.

A scientist made the observation, "This fence isn't necessary. In fact, it's cruel. Children don't need to be fenced in to enjoy their playtime. If we remove the fence, the children will have a more enjoyable time of play. The boundary fence is unnecessary."

The scientists did exactly that. They removed all the playground fencing then sat to observe the children as they played. The results were astonishing. The children didn't run and play as before. Instead, they stayed in a small safe and secure space in the center of the playground. They wouldn't go beyond the eyesight of their teachers or play on the equipment.

The scientists thought this was strange so they decided to put the fence back in place. Immediately, the children begin to utilize all the playground space. They would run to every corner of the playground. What the scientists saw as cruel and unnecessary, the children saw as safety and security.

Kids flourish when boundaries are in place. I know it may seem oppressive but boundaries really do provide more freedom. The absence of rules isn't freedom. It's anarchy. Rules and boundaries provide a safety net for your children to learn and grow as they develop into who they are and who God has created them to be.

We provide our children with boundaries. Some parents call us strict. Others say we aren't strict enough. We have a set of boundaries in place to help our children meet our expectations. Much like the rewards, we don't have a written list or chart of rules and boundaries. We discuss our expectations and then allow our children the freedom to play within these boundaries. They know our expectations and we hold them accountable to meeting our expectations. When a child knows your boundaries, they will excel because they feel safe and secure.

Extraordinary Habit #3 - Responsibility

It's very easy to see that people today don't take responsibility for their actions. Teaching your kids to take responsibility for their actions is an extraordinary habit that will provide the foundation for a lifetime of success.

If you want your children to succeed in life, teaching them responsibility will set them so far above their peers that they'll be unstoppable. They'll always have a job and will always be in high demand. People today are so quick to point the finger and blame others. If you train your children to take responsibility for their actions, they'll be extraordinary!

We live in a world of perpetual toddler tantrums. Every news anchor, movie star, professional athlete, man, woman, or child, when confronted with their behavior says the same thing. "Yeah, I messed up. But at least I'm not as bad as so and so." They point the finger and complain about how bad they've been treated, just like a bunch of screaming toddlers.

No one takes responsibility for their actions any more.

My children aren't perfect when it comes to taking responsibility. Their parents aren't perfect. However, we train them to develop the extraordinary habit of taking responsibility for their actions.

Remember what Ben Franklin said, "It's easier to prevent bad habits than break them." Take responsibility.

Extraordinary Habit #4 – Respect
I'm sure there has always been a contingent of people who don't respect authority. However, the social media landscape celebrates disrespect and has made it the norm.

A lack of respect isn't just on this generation of young people either. You may claim it started with this generation, but a quick glance of any news outlet or social media site proves that people of all ages, from all backgrounds do not respect authority. The modern world celebrates disrespect.

Here's what I've discovered - someone will teach your child respect.

Let that sink in for a moment. Someone will teach your child respect. If we as parents don't teach our children respect, someone in a uniform will do it for you. And most of the time, it's not going to be a pleasant experience for your child. Maybe they'll be taught respect by someone in a school uniform. Such as a principal or teacher. Maybe they'll learn respect from someone in a police uniform. Maybe it will be someone in a gang uniform.

If you don't teach your children respect, someone will do it for you. And if someone in uniform teaches your child respect, it's going to be direct, harsh and absent of love.

Someone will teach your child respect. Let it be you!

Help your kids develop the extraordinary habits of patience, boundaries, responsibility, and respect. In a world filled with average, your children will be extraordinary!

More Good Stuff
Has life ever thrown you a curveball? You won't believe the curveball that hit us late one evening in Memphis! Here's a teaser, it involved one sweet grandmother and one crazy family.

Reflect on the Good Stuff
1. What extraordinary habits do your kids have?

2. What is your go to rug (excuse) of choice?

3. What bad habits have you swept under the rug?

4. What is your plan to correct these bad habits?

CHAPTER 5

Embracing Detours

When you are going through hell, keep going!
—Winston Churchill

When things go wrong, don't go with them!
—Les Brown

One Friday afternoon, we pick our kids up from school and head for Tennessee. We have a speaking engagement outside of Nashville on Saturday evening. The kids are excited because we're going to stop for supper and try a famous BBQ joint in Memphis - The Germantown Commissary. I had eaten at the Commissary a few weeks earlier with some friends and wanted to take the family. I had talked up the Commissary and we're ready for some good BBQ.

We're on the interstate less than ten minutes when Charlie, who was 5 at the time, begins asking the question that parents loathe!

"Dad, are we there yet?"

"No son. We have a three hour drive ahead of us. But how excited are you to eat some BBQ?"

"Super excited! I can't wait!"

This trip is intense. It's raining so hard that I can't see the hood on our car or the lines on the interstate. Traffic is moving at turtle's speed! Our leisurely three hour drive to Memphis turns into a white-knuckled, grip-the-steering-wheel, wide-eyed, muscles-tensed, six hour expedition.

The craziness doesn't stop Charlie from asking his question every ten minutes. "Dad, are we there yet?"

Charlie's constant questioning, coupled with the intense rainstorm, puts everyone on edge.

Finally, after six grueling hours, we make it to the Commissary. We're all excited to get out of the car, stretch our legs, and relax for a bit over a plate of delicious BBQ. As we pull into the Commissary parking lot, we notice it's slammed! Why wouldn't it be? This place is amazing! We circle the parking lot a couple times with no luck. Not one empty parking spot. UGH!

The rain is still coming down in buckets when we spy a parking lot across the busy four-lane highway and decide to attempt to park there. We easily find a spot and realize yummy BBQ is moments away! Then the realization hits us that if we want to eat at the Commissary we will have to run across a four-lane highway with three kids in the pouring rain. We continue to wait, hoping to catch a break in the rain. No such luck.

To everyone's disappointment, we concede that Commissary BBQ isn't going to happen tonight. We want to get out of the vehicle and relax after this tense six hour car ride but will have to wait a little while longer. We wave goodbye and drive in search of another place to grab a late supper.

It's close to 9:30 pm at this point. We find a mall knowing it's sure to be surrounded with places to eat. We eye a sign for a Logan's Steakhouse and a TGI Fridays. Surely, one of them will be have an available parking spot. Logan's it is! We park, race through the rain, and hear the words, "Welcome to Logan's!"

The hostess greets us with a smile, grabs some menus, and walks us to our table. No waiting at all. The hostess informs us that our server will be by in a moment to take our drink order. We smile at each other, breathing a sigh of relief that we made it safely through the rainstorm.

Then we hear it!

Behind us, we hear a commotion of biblical proportion. It sounds as if the Lord reached down from heaven, grabbed all the chairs and tables in Logan's, and hurled them across the restaurant. We spin around to discover an alarming sight.

Thirty to forty grown men and women are going at it! I don't mean they're arguing about he said, she said. I mean they're in a throw-down of the ages. It's a dog pile, fistfight scene you might see in a Western. I'm talking a scuffle that would shame the WWE's Royal Rumble. Grown men and women are throwing punches, slinging chairs, fighting on top of tables. It reminds me of an old cartoon with people fighting in a cloud of chaos. You can't really see anyone, just the occasional foot or arm poking out from the mound of people. Crazy!

We look at each other and can't believe it. What is happening?

Turning back to the chaos, we hear the sweet hostess scream, "Somebody go get Big George!"

Out from the kitchen, stomps the biggest human being I've ever seen. Standing well over six feet tall and weighing in over 350 pounds, Big George emerges from the kitchen, steak tongs still in hand. This guy makes Andre the Giant look small. His arms are the size of most people's legs. His legs are the size of tree stumps. Muscles everywhere! Big George surveys the situation.

Someone screams, "Big George, do something! Break this up!"

Big George responds as only a giant could. He slowly shakes his head side to side to let everyone know that he won't be participating in any part of this foolishness. Big

George slowly turns and stomps his way back to the kitchen.

Just as Big George leaves the scene, an elderly Mamaw yells out, "Oh no! Somebody get the baby!"

A family member on the outside of the dog pile reaches into the pile of people fighting and pulls out an infant still in diapers! Some crazy mother was holding onto her baby with one hand and fighting with the other hand. Thankfully, a family member was able to save the baby from this insanity!

Everyone is in full panic mode at this point. No one knows what will happen next. If one of those folks has a gun, this can turn deadly. Customers race for the exit doors.

I turn to look at my family and their faces are still in shock. Charlie's chin is quivering. He looks at me with the sweetest expression and says, "Father. Father, can we please leave? Can we leave, Father? Please!"

We grab our kids and rush out the door!

We take a few minutes in the car to collect our thoughts. We decide to try one last time to have supper. If TGI Fridays is a bust, we'll be fasting tonight. When the waitress comes to our table, she recognizes that we're all in shock. She sees Charlie still physically shaking from the events. We finish telling her the story just as the lights of the police cars begin flashing at Logan's next door.

It took Charlie two years before he would eat in a Logan's Roadhouse. To this day, we cannot pass by a Logan's without remembering the family brawl. Each of us still hears the words of the Mamaw in Memphis, "Oh no! Somebody get the baby!"

EMBRACING DETOURS

Life is full of detours. A detour is a deviation from the usual or most direct course. A series of unforeseen detours kept us from our plan of a peaceful drive to Memphis to enjoy good BBQ at the Germantown Commissary. We encountered detours of heavy rain, slow traffic, a full parking lot, extra driving, an insane family and one sweet mamaw.

While these detours pale in comparison to the detours we'll face in life; the story does remind us that life is full of detours. How we handle life's detours will ultimately determine our life's destination. We can become bitter at the detours we face in life, or we can embrace these detours and allow them to strengthen us.

Think about Joseph from the Old Testament. His life was filled with detours. He was born into a dysfunctional family. Joseph's dad, Jacob, played favorites. A scheme he learned from his own father, Joseph's grandfather. Jacob gave his son a fancy colorful coat, causing Joseph's brothers to dislike him. Joseph had a dream that revealed he would one day rule over his family, causing his brothers to now hate him. They hated him so much that they devised a plan to fake Joseph's death and sell him into slavery. Their plan worked and Joseph became a slave in Egypt. Joseph's troubles were just beginning. He was falsely accused of attempted rape and thrown in prison. He helped one man legally get out of prison, only to be forgotten about for years.

The Egyptian pharaoh had a dream and Joseph was called from prison to interpret the dream. Joseph properly interpreted the dream for Pharaoh, warning him a famine was coming to Egypt. Pharaoh promotes Joseph to the second highest position in Egypt to prepare Egypt to survive the famine.

During Joseph's term, the famine became so severe that Joseph's brothers traveled to Egypt, seeking food. Through a series of events, Joseph was reunited with his father and family. They survived the famine by living under Joseph's care in Egypt. The detours Joseph faced ultimately allowed his family and the nation of Israel to survive.

If we're honest, most of us wouldn't be able to handle Joseph's life. His life was one horrific detour after another. Sold as a slave. Falsely accused of a crime. Thrown in prison. Forgotten about for years. I'm not sure about you, but I don't believe I'd be able to handle a life filled with this level of disappointment. I would have resolved to live the life of a slave or a prisoner. I wouldn't be looking for, hoping for, or expecting God to use me at all. But that's exactly who God used to rescue his people. A slave. A forgotten prisoner.

Our lives are filled with detours. Sure, our detours may not compare to Joseph's, but we still experience them. Detours aren't planned and seldom produce the outcome we hope for.

I faced a detour while writing this book. After completing the first draft, I printed a copy to proofread and make corrections before sending the manuscript to an editor. When I had only two chapters remaining to proofread, my backpack containing my laptop with the original digital copy and my printed manuscript with the redline edits was stolen when a thief broke into my vehicle.

To say I was devastated would be an understatement. When I realized my rough draft with all my edits was stolen, my heart sank. The blood ran from my face and I became sick to my stomach. All my hard work was gone. All my time, effort, and energy was taken by a petty thief. I was mad!

Thankfully, I had emailed a copy of the rough draft to myself. I didn't have to start completely over from scratch, but it was a major detour. Detours can be devastating. They're unexpected setbacks that derail even our best-laid plans.

When we face a detour in life, we can let it destroy us or define us. We can respond with despair or we can look for ways to use the detour to make us stronger.

Years ago, I read an article about kids who were dealt a detour of sorts in their life. These kids experienced something that altered the course of their lives forever. In essence, their lives were set on a permanent detour. They wouldn't be able to go back to life as normal. They didn't let the detour crush their spirit. Each of these kids embraced their detours by starting a charity to make their communities and the world a better place. Now, if a child can embrace a detour, surely you and I can learn to embrace detours!

Hannah Taylor – The Ladybug Foundation

At the tender age of 5, Hannah noticed a homeless man eating out of a trash can. She decided to take action. By age 8, Hannah had founded the Ladybug Foundation, a charity to help homeless people find food and shelter. Her desire was to assist local charities who work to meet the needs of their homeless population. As of 2014, The Ladybug Foundation has raised over $2 million for the homeless in Canada providing food, shelter, and safety.

On a personal note, I was sharing Hannah's story with a group of young kids in rural Mississippi. After the event, a young woman approached me smiling from ear to ear. She went to school with Hannah in Canada before her family moved to Mississippi. She remembered their school hosting assemblies to help Hannah assemble care packages for The Ladybug Foundation. How cool is that!

You can find out more about Hannah and The Ladybug Foundation at http://www.ladybugfoundation.ca

Alex Scott – Alex's Lemonade Stand

Alexandra, "Alex," was diagnosed with cancer before her first birthday. By the age of 4, she wanted to do something so doctors could help more kids the same way they had helped her. Inspired by the quote, "When life hands you lemons, make lemonade," Alex decided to open a lemonade stand to raise funds for children battling cancer. With the help of her brother, her first lemonade stand raised $2,000.

Unfortunately, Alex passed away at the age of 8, but not before raising $1 million for cancer research. Her parents continue Alex's Lemonade Stand. To date, they've raised over $75 million for more than 375 cancer related research projects.

You can find out more about Alex's Lemonade Stand at http://www.alexslemonade.org/

The Scott Sisters – Sole to Soul

Sisters Vienna, Hayleigh, and Sarah knew they had to do something when they heard of a school fire near Nairobi in Kenya. The images of children walking around with no shoes gave them the idea to purchase shoes to send to the children affected by this fire. The three sisters from New Hampshire went door-to-door asking for shoes they could send to the kids in Kenya.

The sisters raised $33,000 to buy new shoes for 1,500 kids in Kenya. They partnered with Missions of Hope to distribute the shoes to the children in Kenya. Truly from New Hampshire to Nairobi with love!

The Scott Sisters have now partnered with CMF International, a global missions team. To find out more, go to Mohi Sole to Soul Fund. http://give.cmfi.org/p-52-mohi-sole-to-soul-shoe-fund.aspx

Austin Gutwein – Hoops for Hope

At the age of 9, Austin saw a video about children who had lost their parents due to the AIDS virus. He combined his desire to make a difference with his love for basketball and formed Hoops for Hope. On World AIDS Day in 2004, he shot 2,057 free throws to represent the 2,057 children who would be orphaned that day. He received sponsorships for each free throw and raised $3,000, enough to sponsor eight orphans.

Hoops for Hope is now the largest shoot-a-thon in the world. Austin has managed to raise over $3 million for orphans left behind by AIDS. It's estimated that 40,000 people from 25 different countries host their own Hoops for Hope shoot-a-thon each year. Hoops for Hope has raised funds for hospitals, schools, dormitories, computer labs, feeding programs, and water projects. All from a kid who embraced a detour when his eyes were opened to orphans in need.

You can find out more about Austin at http://www.austingutwein.com

Savanna Maxton – Savanna Cares

After sharing these stories with a group of summer camp kids, a mother and daughter approached me. The mom asked if her daughter could share a story with me. That's when I met Savanna. Savanna is a sweet young lady who said, "I want to be able to help missionaries by providing care packages." For several years, Savanna had been raising funds to give to missionaries through her local church. Each year, she would raise several hundred dollars to send to missionaries around the globe.

When she told me this story, I knew we had to share it with everyone at the camp. During our next worship service, I called Savanna to the stage and retold her story. Her beautiful smile brought everyone to their feet, cheering for the young lady who is making a difference in the world.

You can find out more about Savanna on her Facebook page: http://www.facebook.com/SavannaCares

I don't know what your detour will look like. Your detour may come through pain, good fortune, loss of a loved one, kindness from others, heartbreak, or an eye-opening, life-changing experience. I can only promise you that your life will be filled with detours. We can whine, complain, and blame others when the detours come. We can shake our fists at God, asking "Why?" We can say, "It's someone else's responsibility." Or we can learn from these kids and take action.

We must learn to embrace detours and allow them to make us stronger. Detours are almost never planned but can be navigated. And just like our Mamaw in Memphis detour, they usually always make for a great story!

Embrace your next detour by asking, "How can I use this detour to change the world?" The answer just might blow your mind!

More Good Stuff

There's a parenting mindset gaining traction these days that infuriates me! I believe it has the potential to destroy all your hard work as a parent. I'll prove to you that this mindset is dangerous and give you permission to completely ignore it.

Reflect on the Good Stuff

1. What detours have you experienced as a family?

2. How did these detours change your family?

3. What opportunities came about because of these detours?

4. Which of the kid's stories inspired you the most?

CHAPTER 6

Friendship

Kids don't learn from people they don't like.
—Rita Pierson

Scientist are sitting around deciding as always what experiment they should try next. They decide to run an experiment on eight monkeys. First, the scientist place four monkeys in a room. The only thing in this room is a massive tree with a giant bunch of bananas at the top. Everyone knows that monkeys love bananas.

The four monkeys see the bananas and race to the tree. The first monkey stretches to grab the bananas and is sprayed with ice-cold water. You see the scientists had a secret compartment in the wall to spray the monkeys each time they reached for the bananas. The result? The monkey scampers down to the base of the tree.

The second monkey sees the bananas and makes his way to them. Just as he reaches for the bananas, the scientist once again turns on the ice-cold water. The second monkey scampers down the tree.

The third monkey seizes the opportunity to climb the tree. He races to the top, reaches for the bananas and, as you probably guessed, is blasted with ice-cold water. He scampers down the tree faster than the first two monkeys.

The fourth monkey has patiently waited for his opportunity and now races to the top of the tree. Just as he reaches for the bananas, he of course is doused with ice cold water. That's right; he scampers down the tree as well.

This behavior continues until all four monkeys are no longer willing to try for the bananas. They've given up on their dream of eating bananas.

The scientists move to Phase 2 of their experiment.

The scientists replace one of the monkeys with a new monkey. So now, we have three monkeys in the room who have been sprayed with cold water and one monkey who has never been sprayed with cold water.

The new monkey sees the bananas, races to the tree, and begins to climb. That's when the scientist witness something strange. This new monkey is unable to climb the tree because the original three monkeys drag him down. He tries again to climb the tree but is dragged down. Each time he tries to climb the tree, he's dragged down. This behavior continues until this new monkey gives up and no longer tries to reach the bananas.

Next, the scientists remove one of the original three monkeys from the room and bring in a second new monkey. Now we have two monkeys who been sprayed with cold water, one monkey who has never been sprayed with cold water but was unable to climb the tree because he was dragged down, and one new monkey.

The new monkey sees the bananas, races to the tree, and begins to climb. Again, the other three monkeys drag him down. Not just the two original monkeys who were sprayed with cold water, but all three monkeys work together to drag down this new monkey, even the monkey who was never sprayed with water. This behavior continues until this second new monkey stops trying to reach the bananas.

The scientists remove one of the remaining two original monkeys and bring in a third new monkey. Now in the room we have one monkey who was sprayed with cold water, two monkeys who were never sprayed with cold water but were dragged down by the others, and one new monkey.

The new monkey sees the bananas, attempts to climb the tree, and, as you can probably guess, is dragged down. Each time he tries to climb the tree, all three monkeys work together to drag down this new monkey. This third new monkey eventually stops trying and gives up on his dream of reaching the bananas.

Finally, the scientists remove the last of the original monkeys. They replace him with a new monkey. So now in the room we have three monkeys who have never been sprayed with cold water but haven't been able to reach the bananas and one new monkey.

The new monkey sees the bananas. You might think that, since these three monkeys had never been sprayed with cold water, they would allow this new monkey to climb the tree. Wrong!

The new monkey races to the tree excited to reach the bananas. Of course, he is dragged down. Each time he tries to climb the tree, the three monkeys, who were never sprayed with cold water and have absolutely no idea why they're acting and behaving this way, drag this new monkey down. They continue with this behavior until this last new monkey gives up and stops trying to reach the bananas.

I'm sure your heart is aching for these eight monkeys, and I would love to tell you the scientists rewarded all of them with their own truckload of bananas. Unfortunately, the story ends right there. So, let's just say the monkeys were transported to a rainforest filled with delicious bananas where they lived happily ever after.

FRIENDSHIP

I have heard this story many times over the years. It's one of my favorite stories to share with audiences, especially those who work with young people, because it powerfully demonstrates the impact relationships have on people.

I've researched the origins of this story. I'm not sure if this experiment actually took place or if the story was created to teach a greater truth or principle. To me, it doesn't matter if the experiment actually took place or if the story is completely false. The principle behind this story is true. The relationships in our lives matter.

If we surround ourselves with positive-thinking friends, there's a much greater chance we'll think positively. If we're surrounded by negative friends, chances are we'll be negative. If we surround ourselves with friends who love their neighbors, there's a greater chance we'll love our neighbors. Relationships matter.

Just as the monkeys kept dragging the other monkeys down, you can be assured that your kids have people in their lives who are dragging them down. Some mean well. Some probably think they're protecting them from danger. Others have had their dreams crushed by people in their lives so they find it easier to spray cold water on everyone else's dream. They would rather kill your dreams than try anything new.

As parents, we can influence our children's friendship choices. I'll agree that it's much easier to do when our kids are younger, but it's not impossible to do with teenagers. The key to influencing a teenager's friendship choices is to paint a picture for them of what their life will be like if they continue to surround themselves with the wrong types of friends. Author Jim Rohn wrote that we become like the five people we spend the most time with. If your teenager has surrounded herself with five horrible friends, her behavior is most likely going to mirror that of her friends.

Here are eight archetypal friends that we want for each of our kids. Rather than dragging them down, these friends help our kids climb to their highest potential.

Guru
Think Master Shifu from *Kung Fu Panda*. We all need someone who is further along than we are, someone who's been there, done that, so to speak. Personally, I have multiple gurus. Some of these people I know personally and some I only know based on their books, blogs, and videos. Gurus give me business advice, marriage advice, parenting advice, and ministry advice.

Everyone needs a guru. Maybe this is your child's grandparent. Maybe their guru is a teacher or church leader. Help your children identify someone older and wiser that shares your values. A guru will say the same thing you say, teaching your child that you aren't crazy and have their best interest at heart.

BFF (Best Friend Forever)
Think Buzz and Woody from *Toy Story*. We all need a best friend, someone who's by our side through thick and thin, someone who is loyal, dependable, and honest. This person knows us better than anyone else. This can be a classmate, church friend, or neighbor. A best friend will also keep us honest and let us know when we're out of line. Help your child find their BFF. Let them spend time together so they can strengthen their friendship.

Pal

Think Slinky Dog from *Toy Story*. A pal is similar to a best friend but is usually only around during special activities or events in your life. You can have pals at school, church, work, or an extracurricular activity. You may only see your pal a few times a week, month or year but if they are absent, there is a void.

Hero

Think Superman, Batman, Wonder Woman or any of the X-Men. Everyone needs a hero, a real-life hero to look up to. This friend may be an older sibling or parent who courageously says and does the right thing regardless of the personal cost. They stand for what's right even when it's difficult, as they seek to make a difference in their world. Be that hero!

Entertainer

Think Donkey from *Shrek*. We all need a friend who's entertaining. This is a friend you'd bring along for a long car ride. They're the life of the party. They make any activity fun. They're full of incredible stories, have the best jokes, and provide much needed comic relief. These are the people you want in your life when you're down in the dumps. They cheer you up and bring a smile to your face.

Neighbor

Think Wilson from *Home Improvement* or Kramer from *Seinfeld*. This may seem a bit old school, but everyone loves a good neighbor. There's a reason State Farm Auto Insurance continues to use the slogan, "Like a good neighbor, State Farm is there." Your neighbor may live next door, down the street or be from your home town. They are a calm, warm, stable friend who keeps you grounded. A good neighbor will always remind you who you are and where you came from.

Adventurer
This is an Indiana Jones type of friend, someone who will encourage you to take risks and "Live a little!" Life isn't meant to be endured. An adventurer brings life. They bring joy and excitement because they help you experience new things.

Challenger
Think David as he's about to face Goliath. A challenger pushes us to be our best. They see our potential and pushes us toward that potential. This friend believes in you even when the world is against you. When the world is telling you to quit, this friend challenges you to keep going.

It's entirely possible that one person may fill multiple friendship roles. One person may be a BFF, Challenger, and Neighbor. Someone may be an Entertainer and a Pal. You may have two Entertainers and three Heroes. Don't worry if your child is missing one or more of these friends. You can help them identify new friendships.

As a parent, we can fill each of these friendship roles. When they're young, we're their BFF. When we stand for what is right, we are their hero. As they grow, we take them on adventures. We often challenge them. When they're grown with children of their own, we become a guru and pal. Your role will change over time. That's why it's vital to be their parent as well as their friend.

A Dangerous Mindset

Third generation education veteran, Rita Pierson, says, "Kids don't learn from people they don't like." As parents, it's important to be friends with your kids. Parent is not the opposite of friend. These two don't have to be at war with one another.

You can rule with an iron fist and force your kids to obey while they're in your home. This heavy-handed approach will only lead to rebellion when they're out of your home. Your kids have enough people dragging them down and spraying cold water on their dreams. Be the parent and friend who helps them climb.

I want to be friends with my kids. I want to have a friendly relationship with them throughout their entire life. I hate the current parenting mindset, "I'm not your friend; I'm your daddy!" That's dangerous territory to be in as a parent. While I agree that we must parent, remember, kids don't learn from people they don't like.

We've been forced to move twice because of our jobs. Our kids were uprooted from all their friends and classmates. That is, all their friends, except their parents and siblings. I hate to think how my kids would have reacted to each move had they not had a great relationship with their parents. When we moved to a new city, we didn't know anyone. How terrible would it have been for my kids to feel alone in their new home. Being their parent and their friend helped us walk through this difficult transition with our kids.

Help your kids focus on the right friendships. Help them identify and surround themselves with friends who will encourage them to climb to their highest potential. Help them escape the clutches of friends who drag them down and spray cold water on their dreams. If no one else is their friend, you be their friend. You can do it!

More Good Stuff
Now that you've read this far, I feel comfortable sharing an ugly truth. My family is weird, quirky, odd, and different. It's true. Can I let you in on a secret, so is your family! Don't believe me? Ask your BFF to tell you the truth.

The following story will help you understand the importance of celebrating your family's uniqueness.

Reflect on the Good Stuff

Identify the friends in your child's life.

1. Guru

2. BFF

3. Pal

4. Hero

5. Entertainer

6. Neighbor

7. Adventurer

8. Challenger

CHAPTER 7

Your Picture-Perfect Family

Some people are worth melting for.
—Olaf, *Frozen*

Years ago, when I begin traveling with a full-time ministry, I would get extremely bored between speaking events. A two to three-week period between events would drive me bonkers. Anyone who knows me knows that I don't sit well. I'm not a person who's able to sit still for any great length of time. I need a project or activity to consume my mind. A day is one thing, but a week? Two weeks? Torture!

There are only so many times a man can clean the garage, organize the pantry, wipe the kitchen cabinets, or reorganize hall closets. I looked for places in the community to serve. I helped at our local church during the day. I subbed at my kids' school. I needed something to do. Anything to occupy my mind!

One day, while cleaning and organizing our entertainment center, I came across a puzzle given as a birthday present to one of our kids. Finally! Something new! I made my way to the supper table and set out to put the puzzle together.

This was no ordinary puzzle. It was a 1,000-piece mosaic puzzle. A mosaic is a big picture made up of smaller pictures. At a distance, the picture looked normal. Upon closer examination, you could see the smaller images that made up the larger image. This particular mosaic puzzle featured the famous scene of Charlie Brown attempting to kick his football and Lucy pulling it away. Charlie Brown flies in the air and screams "AAUGH!" Each of the puzzle pieces were made up of smaller stills from various Charlie Brown cartoons. This was going to be fun!

I've always loved puzzles. My mom says, as a toddler I had a box filled with various puzzles ranging from 50 to 250 pieces. I would dump all the pieces onto the floor into one giant pile and spend hours putting the puzzles together. The original puzzle boxes were gone so I had to put the puzzles together from memory. I know; I'm a nerd.

I dumped the pieces onto our kitchen table and began to assemble the puzzle. Now, as any puzzle master knows, the first thing you do is turn the puzzle pieces right side up. Next, assemble the border. Then the identifiable images, words, and colors - Charlie Brown, Lucy, the football, and the word AAUGH! I was making great time.

I took a break for lunch with my wife, then quickly got back to the business at hand. With the big images together, I was left with the grass and sky. These two sections were going to be more challenging. The remaining pieces were either green or blue. I started with the grass and had it wrapped up by the time I needed to pick the kids up from school.

Hey, kids! How was school today?

Ethan, "It was great! We got to play dodgeball during PE!"

Maddie, "It was so much fun. My friend and I made up a song with a silly dance"

Charlie, "We read one of my favorite books before nap time."

"What did you do today, Dad?"

"You remember those puzzles we got years ago? The ones that have been in the TV cabinet for years? I started putting one of them together today. I should have it finished before bedtime. You're welcomed to help put it together, but you cannot move a piece off the table. There's nothing more frustrating than losing a piece to a puzzle!"

When we got back to the house, we spent a little time working on the puzzle before making supper. We enjoy eating together as a family. Food is an event in Louisiana! We eat anything. If it doesn't taste good, we salt it until it does, then we eat it.

Yes, we do call it supper. Jesus celebrated The Last Supper not The Last Dinner. I mean if supper was good enough for Jesus, it's good enough for me!

After cleaning the kitchen, the kids and I finished their homework and spent a little time before their bedtime working on the puzzle. At this point, we had less than 100 pieces to go. The end was in sight. After everyone was in bed, I sat down and finished the puzzle. I took a step back, smiled, and left the puzzle for the kids to see the next morning.

They ran to the supper table to see if I had finished the puzzle during the night. We all laughed and smiled at the puzzle. Then one of the kids asked, "What are you going to do with it?"

Such a great question. I've never framed a puzzle before, but this was so colorful that I decided it would look great in one of the kid's bedrooms. Since we have a son named Charlie, it seemed fitting to hang this puzzle in his room. The puzzle looked so great in Charlie's room that we decided to order the remaining three puzzles in the Charlie Brown mosaic puzzle series. All four are now mounted in our kids' rooms.

YOUR PICTURE-PERFECT FAMILY

Let me get this out of the way right now. There is no such thing as a perfect family. It doesn't exist. They all have flaws, imperfections, chips, and cracks. All families have missing pieces: family members who died way too early.

No family is perfect, but they do have some perfect moments. Families are a mosaic. When we look at them from a distance, they all look the same. They look normal. But if we look closer at the day-to-day snapshots of each family, we would see the imperfections, flaws, and missing pieces. We need to focus on OUR picture-perfect family. We do this when we celebrate our family and stop comparing our mosaic to the mosaic of others.

While no family is perfect, they do have some perfect moments. We need to stop comparing one of our family's snapshots to another family's overall picture. We must learn to celebrate the mosaic that makes up our family.

Have you ever noticed that we never compare our family to a family who we think is doing worse than we are? We only compare our lives to those, who in our mind, are doing better than us. Families doing worse than us, we look on with pity. Families doing better than us, we envy.

Remember the movie *Good Will Hunting*. Will is played by Matt Damon, a young man with a troubled past who is constantly in trouble with the law for various misdemeanor crimes such as fighting and disturbing the peace. The thing about Will is that he's a mathematical genius. Through a series of events, he ends up in the care of a math professor at MIT. As a condition of his parole, Will must agree to see a psychiatrist. The psychiatrist he ends up seeing his played by Robin Williams.

There's a scene in *Good Will Hunting* that perfectly illustrates how we need to celebrate the mosaic that is our family. In the movie, Robin Williams plays Sean, a psychiatrist tasked with counseling Matt Damon, aka Will Hunting. Sean is sharing stories with Will about his wife who died from cancer.

It's said the stories in this scene were completely adlibbed by Robin Williams on the spot. The stories are extremely funny and cause Matt Damon to laugh so hard that the directors decided to keep the scene in the movie. After telling these stories, Sean looks directly at Will and says, "My wife's been dead nearly three years, and that's the stuff I remember. Some folks think those things aren't important, but Will, that's the good stuff."

I love that line! "That's the good stuff." It's true! What makes your child unique is what makes them wonderful. What makes your spouse unique is what makes them wonderful. What makes your family unique is what makes your family wonderful. Life is the best when we learn to love our family mosaic. Love your family with all its quirks and idiosyncrasies. Love the family that God has given you.

Too often, we reject our family mosaic wishing it looked like the neighbor's down the street. We covet their house, cars, clothes, gadgets, and hobbies. We secretly want to take pieces from their mosaic and force them into our mosaic.

I know family isn't always easy. Too often, it's filled with difficult and challenging people. I love to tell people the Poland's don't get together unless it's court sanctioned.

But even with these difficult and challenging people, I wouldn't want to do life with any other family.

Here's some things we love celebrate about our family. These may seem silly, but they are the good stuff that makes our family unique.

The Smell

What is it about those first few steps inside the doorway after vacation that makes you realize you're home? It's the smell. It's probably a mixture of your candles, the food you cook, and the people who live there. Every home has an identifiable smell.

The good stuff is walking in and smelling your own home. We love to travel, but we all agree the smell of our house lets us know we're home. There's no place that smells like home.

The Food

What foods does your family enjoy? Is there a meal that makes you feel at home? Growing up, it was my mom's fried chicken. As an adult, there are several meals that remind us of home. We love a good barbecue and my wife's homemade lasagna. What food comes to mind with your family? Makes you want to cook it for supper doesn't it!

That One Piece of Furniture

Every home has at least one piece of furniture that doesn't fit in, but you've had it so long you've named it! Maybe a couch you've had since college. Something homemade that you refuse to get rid of. Maybe the rocking chair you used to rock all your kids to sleep. Or an heirloom grandfather clock that doesn't work. What piece of furniture is in your mosaic?

Traditions

If we were to zoom in on your family mosaic, what traditions would we see? Thanksgiving dinner around the table? Family road trips? A weekend at the lake? Hunting or fishing together? School? Big accomplishments? Small victories? Remember, these simple things really are the good stuff!

The Conversation Starter

For our seventh anniversary, I bought my wife a small clock for our living room. It's been a conversation starter ever since. This is no ordinary clock. Every hour it plays a different musical chime as a set of royal dancers twirl around. When company comes over, they always comment on the clock.

What conversation starter do you have in your home? Something you bought? Something you were given? Maybe it's something you picked up on vacation or a mission trip. Maybe it's something your kids gave you. Every home has a conversation starter. What's yours?

The Collection

Our most visible collection is books. My wife's home office contains a 14-foot-long wall made entirely of built-in bookshelves. It's filled with books we've read and collected over the years. My mother collects whatnots and small figurines. My dad has a collection of artifacts found while farming. My wife's parents collect cast iron cookware and kerosene lamps. What collection is in your mosaic?

Imperfections

The nick in the wall. The doorknob that always gets stuck. The hinge that squeaks. The toilet that always requires you to jiggle the handle. Welcome these imperfections as part of your family mosaic. I know I'm often reminded of our home's imperfections when I receive a Home Depot gift card for Father's Day.

The Never-ending To-do List

The garage that needs to be organized. The gutters that need to be cleaned out. The bushes that need to be trimmed. The flower beds that need to be weeded. Every house has a never-ending to-do list. I'm not suggesting that you be lazy, but there will always be something you could do around your home. Don't allow the to-do list to stress you out and miss spending time with your family.

The Memories

A family mosaic is a collection of memories. My wife and I have our share of heartbreaking memories. We have memories we would rather not endure. Some memories bring tears to our eyes. One memory is of our daughter Elizabeth. She was born very prematurely and lived only three hours. It was an extremely difficult and challenging time for us, but I don't want that memory removed. It's a memory that defines us as a family and makes our mosaic complete. What memories define your family mosaic?

No family is perfect, but they do have some perfect moments. Focus on your picture-perfect family. Your mosaic will be filled with happy, sad, painful, and joyful moments and everything in between. Stop comparing your mosaic to another family's mosaic. Remember the words of Olaf, the snowman from *Frozen*, "Some people are worth melting for." Your family is worth melting for!

More Good Stuff

Late one night my wife heard a stranger in our home. Turn the page to find out who was in our home and why we NOW laugh uncontrollably every time we remember this stranger.

Reflect on the Good Stuff

Let's take a closer look at your mosaic. Who or what comes to mind for each of the following:

1. The Smell

2. The Foods

3. The One Piece of Furniture

4. The Traditions

5. The Conversation Starter

6. The Collection

7. Imperfections

8. The Never-ending To-do List

9. The Memories

<u>CHAPTER 8</u>

Laughter

*A cheerful heart is good medicine, but a
crushed spirit dries up the bones.*
—Proverbs 17:22 (NIV)

Our daughter Maddie was born eight weeks early. She
was very premature and spent the first 21 days of her life
in a specialized wing of the hospital called the neonatal
intensive care unit or what we would come to know as
the NICU.

Those 21 days were intense. Maddie was small, weighing
only 4 pounds 10 ounces. She would fit in the palm of my
hand. Her head would sit on my fingertips with her body
in the palm of my hand and her legs and arms would
dangle off. We came to love all the nurses and doctors at
the hospital who cared for Maddie. Still, to this day,
when we see them, we can't help but hug them, show off
how much Maddie has grown, and how much we thank
them for caring for Maddie.

One of the things we came to learn about the NICU was they kept a very meticulous schedule. We could only visit Maddie at 1:00, 3:00, 5:00, or 9:00 a.m. or p.m. At 7:00 a.m. or p.m., the shift changed when the nurses would go over the details for each of the babies. Visitation was not allowed during shift change. In addition to this visitation schedule, Maddie had other daily schedules. Every three hours, a staff member would wake Maddie to feed her. Every four hours, they would run tests. Every six hours, they would check vital signs. Every eight hours, they would check to see if she was eating, gaining weight, etc.

These various schedules were important because it meant Maddie slept no more than 45 minutes at a time. For the first 21 days of her life, she would go to sleep only to be woken up approximately every 45 minutes by a nurse or doctor coming to check on her. I need to stress the fact that Maddie didn't sleep for more than 45 minutes at a time during her stint in the hospital.

Finally, the day came for us to bring Maddie home. We were, of course, super excited. The nurses told us that we would need to buy a small insert for her car seat because Maddie was so small. Even with this insert, Maddie would still flop around in the car seat. We had to put blankets around her head to keep her upright.

Our friends and family came to visit Maddie once we were home. Everyone had the same reaction.

She so cute. I've never seen a baby so little. She just so cute!

Everyone loved having Maddie around because she was a baby no bigger than a baby doll. Adorable!

Once our friends and family left, we gave Maddie a bath, fed her, and got her ready for bed. We rocked her to sleep and laid her in our bed. Yes, that's right, we allowed Maddie to sleep in our bed. You see, almost a year to the day before Maddie was born, our baby Elizabeth was born so prematurely that she passed away after only three hours. So, now that we finally had our baby girl home, we didn't leave her alone for very long. My wife and I went into the living room, relaxed for just a moment and talked about how happy we were to have our daughter home. Blessed!

Our time of relaxation didn't last long because after 45 minutes, we heard a faint cry coming from the bedroom. Maddie was awake and crying for her parents.

We rushed to the bedroom, scooped her up, brought her into the living room, and rocked her back to sleep. We're all tired at this point, so all four of us decided it was time to get some sleep. The four of us piled into the bed: Mom and Dad on the outsides, Maddie next to Mom, and Ethan next to Dad.

We didn't sleep long, because Maddie only slept for 45 minutes. It didn't bother us because we were so excited to finally have our baby girl home that we eagerly sprang to our feet to calm Maddie down and get her back to sleep. These 45-minutes sleep cycles went on the entire night.

By the time morning rolled around, everyone was spent. Ethan had always slept through the night. So, having a baby that wouldn't sleep was something very new for us. We were tired but the joy of having Maddie home was enough to put a spring in our step, helping us make it through the next day.

I would love to tell you that Maddie quickly adjusted to being home and began to follow the sleep patterns of her older brother, but that would be a vicious lie. Maddie continued this pattern of only sleeping 45 minutes at a time for a year and a half! For the next 18 months, Maddie continued to sleep in 45 minutes intervals. To say that her mom and dad were exhausted would be an understatement. Her older brother quickly realized he could get more sleep in his own bed. So, he moved back to his own bed on the other side of the house.

After 18 months of only sleeping in 45-minute cycles, the excitement of having our daughter home had worn off. We no longer sprang to our feet with joy to comfort Maddie. In fact, when we got up in the middle of the night, we looked and walked like cast members for *The Walking Dead*. We shuffled from place to place dragging our feet as we went along. We were exhausted! Our eyes were bloodshot. Our faces filled with deep crevices. Massive bags under our eyes. We needed sleep!

It was this desperate desire for sleep that forced us to move Maddie to her bedroom on the other end of the house. Ethan's bedroom was next to Maddie's, so with Maddie crying all night, Ethan was back in our bed.

We had tried this a few other times with no such luck. We hoped since Maddie was now 18 months old, putting her in her own bed would solve the problem of her waking up throughout the night. Surely, she would cry herself to sleep. Friends had also offered to keep Maddie for a night so we could get some sleep. But Maddie would cry and scream until she was out of breath which forced us back home each time.

All our foolish plans failed spectacularly!

Maddie continued this 45-minute sleep cycle until the dark night happened.

As we listened to Maddie cry, we realized we were going to have to get up to calm her down. Thus, began the nightly dialogue.

It's your turn to get up

No, it's your turn!

I can't get up; I have to sleep. I have a big meeting tomorrow.

I need sleep. Please get up with her this time.

If you get her this time, I'll get up the next time; I promise.

I must have won the argument this night because Leigh got up and slowly made her way to Maddie's room. The short walk across the house took much longer than normal because we hadn't slept more than 45 minutes at a time for a year and a half. We weren't walking through the house like a mall walker. Think zombie. Think mummy from one of those old classic horror movies. Leigh slowly began shuffling her way to Maddie's room.

It took her so long to get to Maddie that I began having a dialogue with myself. I knew I needed to help, so I made my way to the kitchen to warm-up a bottle for Maddie. My hope was this bottle would allow her to sleep for the rest of the night.

My wife made it back to the bed with Maddie trying her best to calm her down. In her mind, everyone in our home was in our bed. Ethan was next to dad on the far side. My wife didn't realize that I had gone to the kitchen to warm up Maddie's bottle.

Our home was far out in the country surrounded by tall trees. Our road had no streetlamps. When it got dark outside, it was dark! The only hope you had to see anything at night would be if the moon were shining. This particular night, there was a small amount of moonlight casting a dim eerie light through the house.

I finished warming the bottle and began to slowly shuffle my way back to the bedroom. While my wife was lying in the bed, she realized that someone was coming from the kitchen. She knew everyone in the house was in the bed with her. Her women's intuition kicked in and told her that a stranger was in the house.

Leigh peeked over the bed sheets into the kitchen, gazing in the moonlight at the shadowy figure slowly making his way toward the bedroom. She, of course, noticed that this stranger was holding something in his hand. Again, her women's intuition took over to tell her he must be toting a chainsaw! Just as I, this dark shadowy figure, reached the bedroom doorway, my wife let out a scream like I've never heard before. Every part of her body tensed up from her toenails to her tonsils as she screamed out.

RRRRROOOOOAAAAAAAUUUUUUGGGHHHHHHH!

When I heard my wife scream like that, my mind immediately played a terrible trick on me. I hadn't slept in a year and a half, and the devil used my tired mind to play a devious trick. When my wife screamed, the first thought that went into my brain was that we were so sleep deprived that when Leigh made it back to the bedroom she tried to scoot Ethan over and realized we must have been so exhausted that we had rolled over onto him during the night and smothered him to death. I've never heard my wife scream like that, so I knew something terrible must have happened. I honestly thought we had smothered our son.

To any man who may be reading this, I need to ask for your forgiveness. Please don't revoke my man card for what happened next. When I heard my wife scream like I had never heard her scream before and thought that we had smothered our son to death, I screamed! I would love to tell you it was a manly scream. You know, something out of *Braveheart* or *Gladiator*.

No. My scream was nothing like that, not even close. I let out a scream that can best be compared to a small girl screaming at the sight of a spider.

AAAAAAAAAAAAAAAAAAAAAHHHHHHHHHHHHHHHH!

Ethan, after hearing his mom and dad scream simultaneously at the top of their lungs, lifted up on both hands, turned around in the bed, and gave his best Scooby Doo grunt, UUUUGGGGHHHHH!

As you might guess, we were all awake at this point. Our nerves were so shot that we got up and went to the living room to watch TV. There wasn't a whole lot of laughter. My wife sat in the living room thankful that a chainsaw-wielding murderer wasn't in our home. I sat in the living room thankful we hadn't smothered our son to death.

This series of events made us realize we had to get Maddie to sleep through the night. Over the next couple weeks, we were finally able to break Maddie from waking up every 45 minutes. It mainly involved a lot of her crying herself to sleep through the night. The first week, she cried nonstop all night long. ALL NIGHT LONG! I'm telling you, you could hear Lionel Ritchie singing. The second week, she began to cry less and less each night until she finally slept through the night.

LAUGHTER

I've told this story countless times. It always provides several laughs because parents and kids from every culture realize what it's like to be tired, exhausted, and in desperate need of sleep. They know the tricks our minds play on us in our moments of tired desperation.

The Bible equates laughter to medicine. Proverbs 17:22 says, "A cheerful heart (laughter) is good medicine, but a crushed spirit dries up the bones."

Life is absolutely the most fun when we laugh on a regular basis. Our homes need to be filled with laughter. Kids love to laugh. I read a study once that kids laugh, on average, 40 to 50 times a day. Adults laugh, on average, 10 times a day. As adults, we need to laugh more!

I know what you're thinking; I'm not a funny person. That's okay. If you're not a naturally funny person, find someone or something that you and your family enjoys that provides a good healthy dose of laughter. Remember the Bible says laughter is medicine for the soul. Maybe there's a certain comedian that you and your kids can enjoy listening to. Maybe there's a TV show that causes you to laugh uncontrollably. Maybe there's a movie, song, or book that makes you laugh hysterically.

We live in a society that seems to look for ways to be offended. I think we need to relax! I travel and meet folks each week who are amazing. Some rich and some poor. People from every race, creed, color, background, and family scenario you can imagine. All of them are trying to do the best they can for those they love.

Everyone has problems. Some more than others. Face the problems but don't become the face of the problem.

We need to stop allowing news outlets, social media, and hateful people to control our lives. We would be much better off if we turned off the 24-hour news feed and talked to people. If you have people in your life who are bent on dragging you down, remove them from your life.

Life is too short to waste time on negative, hateful people. Life is too long to waste time on negative, hateful people.

Relax. Learn to laugh!

Yes, there's evil in the world. But just because someone has an opinion different than yours, that doesn't make them the devil. I have a diverse group of friends. We don't agree on everything, but we don't allow our differences to destroy our friendships.

Turn off the hate! Turn off the negativity! Stop being offended by everything!

Laugh! Trust me on this, life is so much better and fulfilling when you focus on the good stuff like laughter!

More Good Stuff
Are you rich? I'm not talking about the cash in your bank account, your retirement plan, the number of your material possessions, or the size of your home. There's

nothing wrong with these things. But I'm talking about lasting treasures. The next story perfectly illustrates why we know we're the richest family under the sun.

Reflect on the Good Stuff

1. What movies, songs, comedians, and YouTube videos make your family laugh?

2. What family events or stories from your past have provided countless laughter?

3. What's your family's favorite joke?

CHAPTER 9

Loving Others

*Praise be to the God and Father of our Lord
Jesus Christ, the Father of compassion and the
God of all comfort, who comforts us in all our
troubles, so that we can comfort those in any
trouble with the comfort we ourselves receive
from God.* —2 Corinthians 1:3-4 (NIV)

In the late 1800s, Russell Conwell was a brilliant, entertaining, and motivating pastor. His church Grace Baptist Church was attracting new parishioners at such a rapid rate that the congregation began talking about building a larger meeting space.

During his stint as pastor, a young printer approached Conwell seeking advice on how to enter the ministry. He had no money to pay Conwell, but seeing his ambition, Conwell agreed to tutor the young man. The young printer soon brought a friend to learn under Conwell. Conwell's number of students quickly increased to forty men. Over the next three years, Conwell developed teaching pamphlets and enlisted the aid of volunteers to continue to teach these young men. The idea for Temple

College, now Temple University, was firmly planted in his mind.

Following the Civil War, Conwell gained fame as an orator on the Chautauqua Circuit, a traveling tent show visiting American towns presenting political speeches, spellbinding storytelling, musical performances, and plays. Conwell gave a speech on this circuit entitled the Acre of Diamonds.

No one knows for certain if the tale was true or a parable. Some of Conwell's writings lead me to believe it was a made-up tale he heard from a tour guide during a trip to the Middle East. Whether the story was true or fabricated, it is packed with powerful principles.

By Conwell's own account, he delivered this speech 6,152 times. This fact is even included in Ripley's Believe It or Not. Conwell used the proceeds from his Acres of Diamonds speeches to raise money for Temple College.

The acre of diamonds story begins with a wealthy Persian farmer who learned that diamonds were being discovered in his home country. He desired wealth so he sold his farm and set out to make his fortune in the diamond trade.

He traveled throughout the country, searching the mountains and streams for diamonds. After spending all his money without finding a single diamond, he threw himself into a great tidal wave and drowned.

Meanwhile, back at the farm, the new owner was watering his camel in a stream that ran across the property when a flash of light from the streambed drew his attention. The new owner pulled a curious black stone from the creek admiring how the light reflected all the colors of the rainbow. He took the stone back to his home and placed it on the mantle.

Sometime later, the new owner was visited by a local priest. The priest recognized the black stone as a diamond. In fact, it was one of the largest diamonds ever discovered. He asked the owner where he found the stone.

"The streams on the property are covered with similar stones. Some larger. Some smaller."

Every acre of the farm contained diamonds, making the farm the most productive diamond mine on the entire continent.

Needless to say, the farm the first farmer sold for pennies contained acres of diamonds. If the original owner had simply taken some time to study what diamonds looked like in their natural, uncut state, he would have realized his farm was covered with diamonds.

LOVING OTHERS

I believe each of us has an acre of diamonds right under our noses. I consider my relationship with God, family and friends, and my job my acre of diamonds. It is these things that truly bring happiness and joy to my life.

Too often, we ignore our diamonds because they're hidden, unpolished and look like ordinary rocks. We don't want a diamond farm or diamond mine. We don't want to work for our diamonds. We want the world to hand us polished, cut diamonds. We want the perfect spouse, perfect child, perfect friend, perfect job, perfect everything.

Loving and caring for the people in your life means you treat them like priceless diamonds. If we're willing to look, the diamonds are everywhere.

Here are a few diamonds God has placed in my life.

My Family
Think back to the picture-perfect family chapter. We need to celebrate and love our family. Our family is more valuable than diamonds. Sadly, most of us don't think of our family this way until we're about to lose them. I'm not perfect. I've certainly taken my family for granted. I've ignored them and made them feel devalued. I've trampled on their heart and feelings. Too often, I ignore my family while giving everyone else my full time and attention.

In the face of my shortcomings, I have purposely spent years fighting for my family. Trust me when I say this, your home is full of diamonds!

We must fight for our families. It's so easy today to sell our farm so we can go off exploring new lands in search of something prettier and shinier. The only reason the grass is greener on the other side of the fence is because it receives more fertilizer. What we really need to do is fight for our family!

Here are a few ways that I show love to my wife and kids.

Leigh

My wife's birthday is Christmas day. As you might imagine, her birthday is often overlooked and forgotten in all the hustle and bustle of the Christmas season. For years, I've fought to make her birthday special. Shortly after we were married, I started the Twelve Days of Christmas Birthdays. For twelve days leading up to her birthday, I give her special gifts. Most of them are small, like a Diet Coke and a Zero candy bar, the snack she enjoyed each day after school of our senior year. One year, I gave her a dozen roses, one each day leading up to her birthday. I hid the roses throughout the house and gave her clues to find the day's rose.

Other things Leigh and I do to fight for our marriage is to have regular date nights. Sometimes, we take special trips together without the kids. I love to tell her she's beautiful! More than just telling her, I believe it. The little things really do matter. Fight for your spouse!

My kids

This is nothing new, but kids spell love as T-I-M-E. Spend time with your kids. Be involved in their life.

Attend all their functions that you can: special award days at school, ball games, cheerleader try-outs, and dance recitals. Whatever your kid is into, learn all you can about it! This will speak volumes to them.

Tell them you love them...all the time. We end all our conversations, phone calls, and goodbyes with the words, "I love you!" Our 18-year-old tells his mom and dad, "I love you," even when his friends are around. It's especially important for me to do this with my daughter. I fight hard to be the man I want her to marry. She's twelve and will still hold my hand in a crowded group of her friends. She hugs her parents all the time. Why? Because we spend time with her. We don't view our kids as a nuisance or headache.

Kids also spell love as M-O-N-E-Y. In the Rewards chapter, I shared how we love to reward our kids for behavior we value, but it bears repeating. Spend money on your kids. You don't have to go into debt or mortgage the house, but spend money on them. Cook their favorite meal. Buy them books at the book fair. Let them pick the restaurant. The little things really do matter! Fight for your kids!

Our friends
There is a Bible passage that has become our unwritten family motto. We don't have it plastered on the walls. In fact, it's not found anywhere in our house, cars, desk drawers, or night stands. We've talked about it over the

years and it has come to silently guide us as we interact with the world around us, especially our friends.

"Praise be to the God and Father of our Lord Jesus Christ, the Father of compassion and the God of all comfort, who comforts us in all our troubles, so that we can comfort those in any trouble with the comfort we ourselves receive from God. For just as we share abundantly in the sufferings of Christ, so also our comfort abounds through Christ. If we are distressed, it is for your comfort and salvation; if we are comforted, it is for your comfort, which produces in you patient endurance of the same sufferings we suffer. And our hope for you is firm, because we know that just as you share in our sufferings, so also you share in our comfort." 2 Corinthians 1:3-7

2017 marked a milestone for the Poland clan. Our oldest son, Ethan, graduated high school. We've always said since he was born, if every baby were like Ethan, the world would be full of kids. He's always been a joy and blessing in our life. Seldom sick. As tough as they come. He's a very determined young man. We pointed him in the direction of his God-given gifts and watched him excel. Truth be told, he's an all-around better man than I am. I cannot wait to see what he accomplishes in his life.

Over the last few months of his senior year, the parents of the graduates were encouraged to provide breakfast to the senior class. Leigh and I wanted to do something special for this senior class. After tossing around several options with our friends, we settled on the idea of a hot and cold breakfast. We would cook sausage, eggs, boudin (a Louisiana sausage made with rice and pork) and provide a cereal bar stocked with all their favorite childhood cereals. To top it all off, my wife decided to make her famous, ooey-gooey, unbelievably delicious homemade cinnamon rolls.

While discussing this breakfast with some friends, we discovered their kids had been sick all week. My wife and I decided to make a couple extra pans of cinnamon rolls to deliver to each house on our way to the senior breakfast.

We made it to the school and began cooking for Ethan's senior breakfast. The bell rang and we saw the students making their way to the breakfast area. The kids were absolutely amazed at the smorgasbord of breakfast items. Everyone filled their plates and sat down to relax with their friends around the tables. Several of them came back for seconds; a few even came back for thirds

We noticed it was time for them to go back to class, so we told Ethan it was time to head back. They said their teacher was out today so they didn't have to rush back. It helped that their sub was enjoying the breakfast as well. The class spent most of their class period eating breakfast and hanging out. It was a great morning.

If we were being honest, it would've been much easier to get doughnuts or Chick-fil-A chicken biscuits, but this isn't how our mind works. We have nothing against those breakfast items, but we chose to do something a little special for Ethan's senior breakfast. Remember the little things really do make all the difference.

Maybe you don't make cinnamon rolls. What do people in your life need most? What's a way you could show love and serve those in your sphere of influence? Could you make them a meal? Could you watch their kids so they could go out on a date? Love others! It always works.

Our acquaintances

We're all creatures of habit. We tend to go to the same restaurants, shops, grocery stores, and shopping centers. We make a point to get to know the people who work in the businesses we frequent. Some are the owners. Others are the cashiers or wait staff. People who work with the public have to deal with some of the rudest, craziest, mean-spirited people on the face of this Earth. They're mistreated, talked down to, and often thought of as merely servants at the customer's beck and call. We make a special effort to try to brighten the day of our regular acquaintances.

Maybe you've never thought about bringing joy to the acquaintances in your life. We do and we love it! We love the owners of our local donut shop. They're from Cambodia. They're the sweetest most generous people! We love the waitress at our favorite sushi restaurant. We request her table every time. She remembers what we like to drink, what we like to add and take away from our entrees. Once when we couldn't sit in her section because it was packed, she corrected our order from the back because she knows what we always order. That's awesome!

Here are a couple ways you can love the acquaintances in your life.

Smile. Let them know you're happy to see them. Ask about their family. Find out their hobbies. Build a relationship with them. Will this take some time? Absolutely. But it's worth it. Remember, you are looking for diamonds that will make your life complete.

We love to joke and kid with our acquaintances, especially if we notice that they've had a rough day. Helping someone smile and laugh will ease their stress. It can defuse a tense situation and make their day.

Once at a hotel's continental breakfast, I noticed an elderly gentleman standing off the side, waiting to bus the tables. He wasn't smiling. He wasn't frowning either, for that matter. He was there physically but his mind was someplace else. I noticed he was wearing an Ohio State Football shirt. I don't recommend this approach for everyone because it can backfire if you don't say this with the right tone and facial expression. I went up to him, patted him on the shoulder, grinned, and said, "Sir, if this hotel won't give you a better shirt to wear while you're working, I'll be happy to file a formal complaint so we can get you a better uniform."

His whole attitude changed. He perked up, laughed, and responded, "Well what team should I be wearing?"

We were at this hotel three days. Every morning, this man greeted us with a smile and gave us some of the best recommendations for local restaurants, shopping, and hangouts. All because, I noticed someone who looked like he needed a pick me up.

The acquaintances in your life are the good stuff. Life is so much more fun when you focus on others.

Our work
Another diamond we celebrate is our work. We've had all challenging jobs. Years ago, we began to tweak how we talked about our work. We began to say, "I GET TO go to work" rather than "I've GOT TO go to work."

A "get to" attitude is grateful. Gratitude is one of the healthiest attitudes we can possess. Having a grateful attitude will reduce stress and aggression while improving your self-esteem, sleep, and your physical, mental, and psychological health. Gratitude increases your likability. People love to be around grateful people.

There is always something to be thankful for. Always! Even in difficult or temporary jobs, you can be grateful. Begin to say, "I get to go to work" rather than "I've got to go to work!" It won't always be easy, but it will be worth it. This will fill your life with joy.

I know it may seem unimportant to think of the relationships in your life in terms of diamonds. God was the first to say, "It isn't good for man to be alone." We're built for relationships. Hopefully, you've identified some diamonds in your life. They've been hidden right under your nose. Just as real diamonds are formed over time with pressure, heat, and cutting. The diamonds (relationships) in your life will take time to form but they are worth fighting for because they are one of the few things in this life that are eternal. Life is so much more joyful and fun when we fill it with diamond relationships and attitudes.

More Good Stuff
You're almost done. You've learned to celebrate your family mosaic, reward behavior you value, laugh, and surround yourself with friends who will help you climb.

However, without the final chapter, life is meaningless. Sure, you may have some fun moments, but those moments will quickly fade. The following chapter is absolutely essential to living an abundantly full life!

Reflect on the Good Stuff

1. What diamonds has God placed in your life?

2. How do you show love to:
    - Your spouse?

    - Your kids?

    - Your friends?

    - Your acquaintances?

3. Have an attitude of gratitude. Over the next week, begin to say, "I GET TO go to work" rather than "I've GOT TO go to work." List everything you like and appreciate about your job. Reflect on this list each morning before heading to your job.

CHAPTER 10

The Gift of God

For God so loved the world that he gave his one and only Son, that whoever believes in him shall not perish but have eternal life. For God did not send his Son into the world to condemn the world, but to save the world through him. Whoever believes in him is not condemned, but whoever does not believe stands condemned already because they have not believed in the name of God's one and only Son. This is the verdict: Light has come into the world, but people loved darkness instead of light because their deeds were evil. —John 3:16-19 (NIV)

But God proves His own love for us in that while we were still sinners, Christ died for us!
—Romans 5:8 (NIV)

My family loves to travel together and encourage others by bringing fun, joy, love, and laughter to people from every walk of life. But it's not only about fun and jokes. We also love to share the life-changing message of Jesus Christ. The gospel of Jesus Christ is the best of the good stuff. Life wasn't meant to be endured. Jesus said in John 10:10, "I have come that you may have life and have it to the fullest." The only way to live life to the fullest is to live it for Christ.

This is one of our favorite ways to share the gospel. Volumes have been written on this topic. This isn't meant to be an in-depth explanation of the gospel. That being said, this is one of the most popular ways I share the gospel of Christ with kids and adults.

John 3 is one of the most commonly known passages in the Bible. Jesus is visited by Nicodemus, a Pharisee who was a member of the ruling council of Jerusalem. Nicodemus asks Jesus what someone must do to be saved. Jesus tells Nicodemus, "God so loved the world that he gave his one and only Son so that whosoever believes in him, would not perish, but have eternal life."

God is our Heavenly Father. He loves us and wants to be in a relationship with us. In fact, he desires a relationship with us so much that he allowed his Son, Jesus, to be sacrificed for your sin and my sin. I have three children and would gladly give my life to save them. If our house was on fire, I believe I would do everything within my power to save them from the fire.

If you were visiting during the fire, I don't know that I'd risk my kids' life to rescue you from the fire. I would attempt to rescue you, only after I have saved my own children. But God loves you so much that he allowed his Son to die so that you could live. Now that's love!

John 3:16 isn't the end of the story. While God freely gave his Son so that we may have eternal life, there's a problem. In verse 19, Jesus tells Nicodemus "light has come into the world, but men love darkness." Darkness is a metaphor for sin. In this passage, Jesus is telling Nicodemus that He's the light that God sent into the world to rescue men from their sins.

The problem is that not everyone accepts God's free gift of salvation. Our hearts love sin, which has caused our hearts to grow hard as stone toward the gospel. People have reasons and excuses for rejecting the gospel. While God doesn't overlook our reasons and excuses, it's helpful to look at a few of the common reasons people give for rejecting the gospel of Christ.

No Love
Some people reject that gospel of Christ because they've never experienced love. They question whether God really loves the world when they've never experienced love. Their parents don't love them like they should. Their grandparents don't love them. Their friends at school don't love them. Since they've never experienced love here on earth, they find it difficult to accept that God could love them.

Maybe this is you. Maybe your parents don't give you the love you need. Maybe your grandparents, your friends, your teachers, your neighbors haven't shown you the love that you feel you deserve. Maybe this has caused your heart to grow hard as stone making it difficult for you to accept the gospel of Christ. Rather than allowing God to renew your heart, your heart of stone rejects the gospel of Christ.

Bad Stuff
Some people reject the gospel of Christ because they see bad stuff in the world. They look at the world and see people hurting, natural disasters destroying people's homes, friends who move away, and loved ones who pass away too soon. When these people see the world, all they see is bad stuff.

Maybe this is you. Maybe you've been hurt by someone close to you. Maybe something bad happened to you or your family that was totally not your fault. Maybe you had a loved one die. When you see the world filled with bad stuff, you question the existence of loving Heavenly Father. You think, "If God truly loved the world, He wouldn't allow bad stuff to happen." Rather than allowing God to renew your heart, your heart of stone rejects the gospel of Christ, because all you see around you is bad stuff.

My Way
Some people reject the gospel of Christ because they want to do life their way. They don't want anyone telling them what they can or cannot do. They don't want anyone telling them what's right or wrong. They don't want anyone telling them anything. "It's my way or the highway!"

This was the group I belonged to. I didn't grow up in a church home, so frankly, I didn't give the gospel a second thought. I didn't want anyone telling me what I could or couldn't do. I wanted to live life my way. Looking back, I simply refused to allow God to renew my heart of stone.

Maybe this is you. Maybe you're like I used to be. You don't want anyone telling you what you should or shouldn't do. No one will tell you how to live. So, when someone shares the gospel with you, you simply don't care to hear it. It's your way or the highway. No one can tell you anything! If you're like I used to be, you simply reject and ignore the gospel of Christ.

The Good News

Romans 5:8 says, "But God proves His own love for us in that while we were still sinners, Christ died for us!" This means that while we were sinners with hearts of stone toward his Son and the gospel, deserving death, God proved what he said in John 3:16. He proved his love for us, by allowing Christ to die for our sins. Romans 5:8 doesn't say, "God proves His own love for us in that while we were perfect and sinless, Christ died for us." Just the opposite. By allowing Christ to die for sinners, people with hearts of stone toward him, God proved his love by allowing Christ to die for our sins. That's Good News!

John 3:17 drives the point home of God's love. "For God did not send his Son into the world to condemn the world, but to save the world through him." A lot of people believe God sent Jesus to only condemn and destroy the world. It is true that the world will ultimately experience God's judgement. However, John 3:17 is clear, God sent

Jesus into the world to save the world so we could have an eternal relationship with him.

You see, Jesus came to give us a new inside, not a new outside. God sent Jesus to die for us, to remove our heart of stone and replace it with a new heart. Jesus came to give us a new heart, one that longs to please the Father and loves the things that he does.

The Choice
The Good News is that God loves you, wants a relationship with you, and offers salvation through Christ as a free gift to you. It's a free gift to everyone. As with any gift, you must choose to accept it. You can choose to continue living with a heart of stone or choose to accept God's free gift of salvation through Christ.

If you would like to accept God's free gift of salvation, simply bring your hands together, bow your head, and call out in faith to God.

Dear God,

I ask you to forgive me of my sins. Give me a new heart. One that longs for and loves the things that you do. Surround me with friends who will keep me strong and focused on you. Thank you for sending Jesus to die for my sins. I am putting my faith and trust in Christ.

I ask all this in Jesus' name.
Amen

These are not magical words. As the ole preacher says, "Saying these words no more makes you a Christian than standing in a garage makes you an automobile." The power is in the finished work of Christ. Ephesians 2:8 tells us that we're saved by grace through faith. Based on the word of God, in 2 Corinthians 5:17, if you prayed this simple prayer of faith, you're a new creation. The old you is gone and the new you is here.

If you asked Christ into your life, let me add that Jesus never promised that your life would be easy and free of pain. Jesus says, "In this world you will have trouble." Some people wrongly believe that Christians will never face difficulty, but that belief isn't based on Scripture. What's promised is that Christ will be with you through every challenge and difficulty you'll face in life. Hebrews 13:5 reminds us that God will "never leave you nor forsake you." 1 Peter 5:7 begs us to cast "all our anxiety (or cares) on him because he cares for you."

Not long after my wife and I become Christians, we faced one of the most difficult challenges a young married couple could face. We were pregnant with our first daughter Elizabeth. Around the twentieth week of pregnancy, my wife began to experience terrible abdominal pain. By the time we were able to see our doctor, it was too late. Our daughter Elizabeth was born twenty weeks premature. She lived three hours. We were devastated. It was one of the most difficult times of our lives. While the pain and heartache was unreal, the peace we experienced from God through this time was real and tangible. God extended more grace and peace to us than we could have imagined. He provided people in our lives in the days and weeks that followed at the time we needed them most.

Two weeks after Elizabeth was born, Leigh and I were at one of our lowest points. We met for lunch and were wallowing in our heartache. In walked Mr. Ray Walters, our neighbor at the time. He talked to us for over an hour. He never sat down. He just stood by the table and loved on us. What makes this story so unbelievable is when Mr. Ray said, "JoAn (his wife) and I only come to town once a month for lunch. We were just here last week, but she sent me here to get some lunch to take back home."

You may have missed that. We did not! We knew without question that God had prompted the Walters to come for lunch at the very restaurant on the very day Leigh and I were at our lowest. God sent just the right person to cheer us up. God will do the same for you. When you feel you're at your lowest in your darkest hour, God will send a Mr. Ray just for you.

Let me also say that God loves you and wants a relationship with you more than you could ever know. He wants to be in relationship with you so much that he was willing to allow his Son to die for you. I encourage you to seek after God and you will find him. The Creator of all life wants a relationship with you. This is the best true story of all!

I don't know what you're going through in this life. I can only promise you that God loves you and wants a relationship with you. If you are not a Christian, I hope that you will seek out someone to answer any questions you may have.

Reflect on the Good Stuff

1. If you prayed this simple prayer of faith, I encourage you to become an active, faithful member of a local Bible-believing church. I am certain your community has several great churches. Get plugged in!

2. Make a commitment to read the Bible on a regular basis. It's filled with true stories of real men and women who faithfully served God with all their heart. There's a myriad of free podcasts that can also help you as you grow in your faith.

3. Find someone to be your accountability partner to encourage you on your journey. I have several men who hold me accountable in various areas of my life.

4. If you're a believer, I pray that this chapter gave you a fresh look at Jesus Christ our Savior. Salvation truly is the greatest gift of all!

FOR GOD DID NOT
SEND HIS SON INTO
THE WORLD TO CONDEMN
THE WORLD, BUT TO
SAVE THE WORLD
THROUGH HIM

John 3:17

__Conclusion__

Don't Blink!

You've made it to the end of the book and are probably asking, "Does this stuff really work?" "Will these simple stories and their principles really make a difference in my home?" "Why should I try this in my home?"

Don't blink!

That's right. Don't blink! Don't blink because when you do your kids will be graduating preschool, graduating middle school, graduating high school, graduating college. You will blink and one day your kids will be gone from your home building their own life and family.

My mom keeps a laminated newspaper article on her fridge. This article has been on the fridge as long as I can remember. The title is *When the Children Grow Up*. The author says, "When the kids grow up then you will organize the rooms, make the beds, and have the house clean. You will prepare the perfect meal and eat it alone. The only thing left is a voice crying, 'Why don't you grow up!' And the silence will echo, 'We did.'" My mom underlined that last line. It's so true. Time flies.

One day our kids will be grown up and gone. I don't want to regret a single minute of the time I have with my kids. I don't want to waste it focusing on all the wrong things. Pick and choose your battles.

Start today focusing on the good stuff! There is always something to be thankful for. Focus on the good stuff!

One reason our friends consider our family a happy family is that we don't stress out about the small stuff. We don't gag at gnats. Our kids don't rule the roost and our house is not a pigsty, but we don't stress when toys are left in the yard overnight. We don't stress if footprints get on the flooring. We don't stress if the laundry isn't completed each day. We pick our battles. These are simply not battles that we choose to fight every minute of every day.

Enjoy the different stages of life with your kids because, in the blink of an eye, they'll be gone. It seems like yesterday that we brought Ethan home from the hospital. Then we blinked and he graduated high school. I want to encourage you to spend time with your family. Reward your kids for behavior you value. Life is more fulfilling when you focus on the good stuff.

Maybe you've experienced loss. Maybe you need to forgive yourself, forgive your child, and bury the bad behavior in the sea of God's forgetfulness. Maybe you need to forget it and move on. Maybe you could start by taking some cinnamon rolls to a neighbor down the street. Maybe you need to help your son or daughter with their friendship choices. Or maybe you simply need to begin to celebrate the mosaic that is your family.

Fight for your family. You can make a difference. There are no perfect parents. Remember, Mary and Joseph left Jesus at the temple for several days before realizing he was missing. I doubt you have forgotten about your kids for a week. So, keep your head up! You're making a difference.

Don't give up. Don't stop trying. Don't stop loving and fighting for your family. The simple stories I shared in this book will help you and your family live a fuller life. They work in our home. I know they'll do the same for you.

You're making a difference!

Don't give up!

You're doing a great job!

Keep fighting for your family!

I believe in you!

It is worth it!

Ain't life fun, when you focus on the good stuff!

ABOUT THE AUTHOR

Clayton Poland is a talented evangelist, speaker and entertainer who travels nationally and internationally bringing the Bible to life for this generation. He is an ordained minister with a passion for this generation. He believes this generation, young and old alike, can and will do great things for the Kingdom of God. Clayton lives in West Monroe, Louisiana with his wife Leigh and their three kids; Ethan, Maddie and Charlie.

You can find out more about Clayton by visiting his website www.ClaytonPoland.com.

ADDITIONAL PARENT RESOURCES

Parent Parables empower parents to help them overcome just about every issue they may face. Each week you will receive a video containing simple practical parenting wisdom.

To find out more about Parent Parables;

Text: Parables
To: 44222

<u>FREE LEADERSHIP RESOURCES</u>

Leadership Extras is a free resource providing leaders a weekly illustration, story, statistic or team building exercise to help you drive home your message or presentation.

To find out more about Leadership Extras;

Text: Extras
To: 44222

Invite Clayton to your next event!

Clayton is a talented evangelist, speaker and entertainer who encourages audiences to focus on the good stuff. His events combine fun, family friendly humor, encouragement and life-changing truth. His down-home delivery coupled with his energetic style and unbelievable stories reaches people of all ages from all walks of life.

An evening with Clayton Poland will leave you shouting, ain't life fun...when you focus on the good stuff!

For more info, go to www.claytonpoland.com

94748782R00095

Made in the USA
Columbia, SC
06 May 2018